Buildings of St Kilda

CW00819199

Buildings of
St Kilda

Geoffrey P Stell

Mary Harman

THE ROYAL COMMISSION
ON THE ANCIENT
AND HISTORICAL
MONUMENTS
OF SCOTLAND
1988

The Royal Commission on the Ancient and Historical Monuments of Scotland

CONTENTS

Village; street from E

vii   Preface

viii   Abbreviations used in the references

ix   Editorial Notes

1   Introduction: Settlement and Buildings

1   Historical Evidence

15   Evidence of Field Survey

15   i   Village: Settlement

17   ii   Village: Estate and Community Buildings

19   iii Village: 19th-century Houses

21   iv   Village: Early Houses and Structures

23   v   An Lag Bho'n Tuath

25   vi   Gleann Mór: Settlement

27   vii Gleann Mór: Structures

28   viii Cleitean and Bothies

31   Population Evidence

33   Notes

35   Descriptive List

55   St Kilda, the National Trust for Scotland
       and the World Heritage Convention

57   Glossary

57   Index

       Map in end-pocket

v

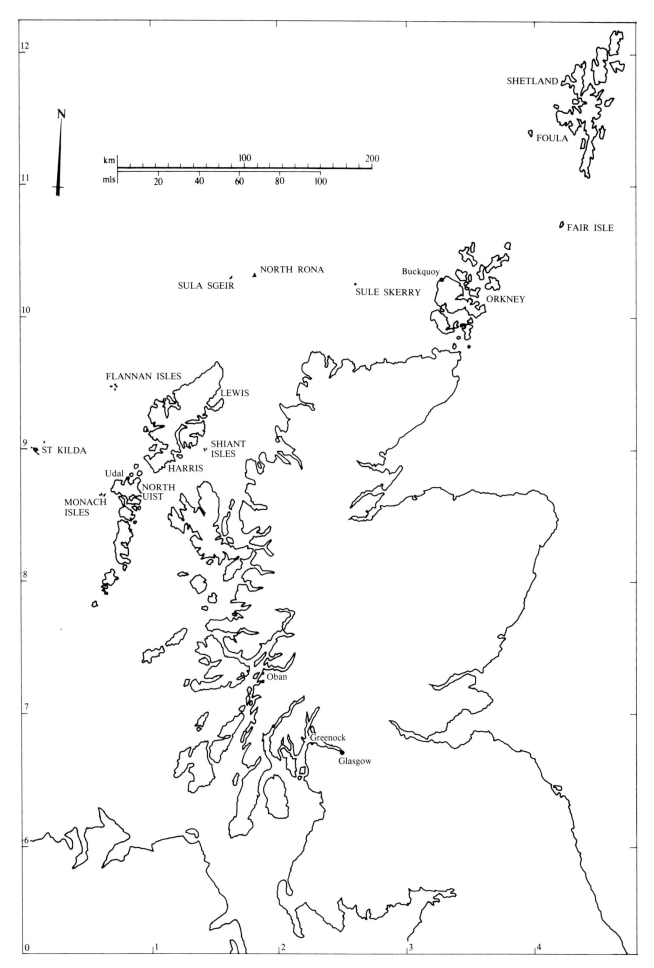

Scotland showing St Kilda and other comparable islands and sites

PREFACE

This volume forms part of a series of occasional publications designed to give fuller treatment to subjects which cannot be embraced within the normal course of the publication programme of the Royal Commission on the Ancient and Historical Monuments of Scotland. It embodies the results of a detailed survey of the main areas of historic settlement on St Kilda carried out by the Commission in 1983–6 at the invitation of the National Trust for Scotland, the owners of this group of islands. It also incorporates some of the findings arising from the field surveys and research conducted by Mary Harman throughout the archipelago since 1977.

Although much has been written about St Kilda, there is no work wholly dedicated to the buildings and antiquities of the islands, which received only cursory treatment in the Commission's *Inventory of Monuments in the Outer Hebrides* published in 1928. The Commissioners have therefore taken this opportunity of making good the gap in the official record and at the same time have endeavoured to provide a concise guide to these aspects of the islands' history. This volume is also intended to pay tribute to the considerable importance and interest of St Kilda, reflected in its recent inclusion in the World Heritage List.

The remote and scenically spectacular islands of the St Kilda group lie sixty-four kilometres W of North Uist in the Outer Hebrides, and represent one of the most distant outposts of human settlement in the British Isles. Their name is almost certainly a mistranscribed and misapplied version of the Old Norse *Skildir* (shields), which on some early maps appears to have been associated with one of the offshore islands closer to the main Hebridean chain. The Old Norse *Hirtir* (stags) and its derivative forms constitute a more authentic historical title, but nowadays the name Hirta tends to be restricted to the largest island of the archipelago, the other main islands being Soay, Dùn and Boreray with its grand attendant stacks.

The historical record of human settlement on St Kilda is largely confined to the last three centuries and is of an episodic nature, relying heavily on accounts by travellers and resident or visiting ministers. It is with the structures of these centuries that the present study is mainly concerned. Martin Martin's visit in 1697 produced the first full-length account, and among the most significant of the later descriptions are those by the Reverend Kenneth Macaulay, who visited St Kilda in 1758, the first year of his ministry, and by the Reverend J B Mackenzie, who wrote about the improvements carried out by his father, the Reverend Neil Mackenzie, minister on St Kilda from 1829 to 1843. Mackenzie's incumbency witnessed a major transformation in the form and pattern of settlement in the village on Hirta, and a further programme of house-building was undertaken in the 1860s. Thereafter, descriptions and pictures chart the decline of the island community which led eventually to the evacuation of the last thirty-six inhabitants in August 1930. A transformation of a different kind has taken place since 1957, for St Kilda then became the site of a permanent military base housing a unit of the Royal Artillery detached from the garrison of the Guided Weapons Range on Benbecula; it has also become the scene of regular seasonal activities on the part of the National Trust for Scotland and the Nature Conservancy Council.

The activities of the past 150 years and the islanders' distinctive ways of life are faithfully reflected in the physical remains of human settlement, especially within the area of the village on Hirta. However, it is less easy to identify surviving traces of building-types mentioned by earlier commentators, or to assign precise dates to those remains for which a greater antiquity has been claimed. Further examination of such structures must, in the absence of any coherent historical record, proceed purely on an archaeological basis, and although they have attracted much attention, particularly in recent decades, a thorough overall survey of the archaeology of these islands remains long overdue. This assessment of the standing buildings and other structural remains of the historic period on St Kilda is thus presented as a first contribution to such a survey.

The text has been written by Geoffrey Stell and Mary Harman, whose assistance in compiling this material and sharing the results of her own independent survey work has been much appreciated. The survey-drawings which form the core of this work are by Alan Leith, Ian Parker and Sam Scott, and, except where otherwise stated, the modern photographs have been taken by John Keggie. The survey was coordinated and the volume edited by Geoffrey Stell; the book has been designed by Ian Scott and John Stevenson, and Elizabeth Shaw did the typing.

For the help and advice that they have received, the members of the survey team wish to record their gratitude to their colleagues, especially Jim Davidson, Ian Fleming, Graham Ritchie and Jack Stevenson; to the National Trust for Scotland and the St Kilda Club, particularly Alexander Bennett, Philip Schreiber and members of various St Kilda Work Parties; to the Nature Conservancy Council and their wardens, David Miller, Peter Moore, and Wally Wright; to members of HM Armed Forces, St Kilda Detachment; to the University of Durham, Department of Archaeology, especially Christopher Morris, Colleen Batey and Norman Emery; to Meg Buchanan, Dorothy Kidd, Bill Lawson, Margaret Mackay, Stuart Murray and Isabel Steel.

For permission to reproduce material, acknowledgements are also due to Sir Richard Dyke Acland; Robert Atkinson; Bill Lawson; the National Library of Scotland; the Royal Museum of Scotland; the School of Scottish Studies, University of Edinburgh; and Stirling Reference Library.

ABBREVIATIONS USED
IN THE REFERENCES

Buchanan, *Album*
—Buchanan, M, *St Kilda, A Photographic Album* (1983).

Lawson MS
—Lawson, W, *St Kilda* (Unpublished typescript; copy
    available on restricted access in National
    Monuments Record of Scotland).

Macaulay, *History*
—Macaulay, K, *The History of St Kilda* (1764).

MacCulloch, *Western Islands*
—MacCulloch, J A , *A Description of the Western Isles of
    Scotland* (1819).

MacCulloch, *Highlands*
—MacCulloch, J A, *The Highlands and Western Isles of
    Scotland* (1824).

Mackenzie, *Life*
—Mackenzie, J B (ed.), *Episode in the Life of the Rev. Neil
    Mackenzie at St Kilda from 1829 to 1843* (1911).

Martin, *Voyage*
—Martin, M, *A Late Voyage to St Kilda* (1698; edition of
    1753 reprinted 1970).

Monro, *Western Isles*
—Munro, R W (ed.), *Monro's Western Isles of Scotland
    and Genealogies of the Clans 1549* (1961).

NLS
—National Library of Scotland, Edinburgh.

PSAS
—*Proceedings of the Society of Antiquaries of Scotland.*

Small, *Handbook*
—Small, A (ed.), *A St Kilda Handbook* (1979).

Williamson, *Summer*
—Williamson, K, and Boyd, J M, *St Kilda Summer* (1960).

EDITORIAL NOTES

Editorial conventions follow practices adopted in the Commission's standard publications. Notes and references will be found at the end of the Introduction and following each article. Those notes that include additional information are indicated in the text by an asterisk.

The Descriptive List comprises articles on a selection of thirty significant or specimen structures that have been recorded and analysed in detail; the numbers of these articles are cited in bold throughout the volume. The heading of each article includes the National Grid Reference of the building concerned and the National Monuments Record of Scotland record card number. The precise date of survey is not given, but all surveys were undertaken between 1983 and 1986. A glossary of special or technical terms will be found near the end of the book.

Illustrations are treated as Figures and are integrated with the text. Where there are two or more illustrations on a page of the Introduction, individual Figures are distinguished by letters; illustrations accompanying the Descriptive List bear the number of the article to which they refer, with a letter suffix if the article is illustrated by more than one Figure.

Except where otherwise specified, the contents of this book are Crown Copyright; copies of the photographs and drawings can be purchased, on application to:

The Secretary,
The Royal Commission on the Ancient and
   Historical Monuments of Scotland,
54 Melville Street,
Edinburgh, EH3 7HF.

For ease of reference and identification, all except unique estate or community structures on St Kilda have been assigned numbers or letters which are marked on the accompanying plans. As has been customary for some time, the houses erected in the 1860s are referred to by number, the sequence from House 1 to House 16 running E–W from Abhainn Ilishgil (the Dry Burn) to Abhainn Mhór. In the absence of other indigenous forms of address, the black houses of the 1830s have been given a corresponding sequence of letters from A to V, while Black Houses W–Z are located in the area between Abhainn Ilishgil and the glebe wall. In and around An Lag Bho'n Tuath a series of structures recorded by M B Cottam are given a C prefix and number. For structures in Gleann Mór, other than the small storage buildings known as cleitean, however, the system of reference-letters introduced by K Williamson and I M Boyd has been adopted and extended in preference to the numerical sequence later applied by Cottam and published in Small, A (ed.), *A St Kilda Handbook* (1979), 54. The correlation of the Williamson letters (additional letters cited in parentheses) and Cottam numbers for structures in Gleann Mór is as follows:

A	11	E	1	I	5	M	19	(Q)	7
B	12	F	3	J	6	N	15	(R)	8
C	13	G	4	K	17	O	16	(S)	10
D	2	H	9	L	18	P	14	(T)	20

Cleitean throughout the archipelago are identified by a single series of numbers originating from those assigned to village cleitean and cleit-like structures by J M Boyd and P A Jewell (for the purposes of studying Soay sheep) in the early 1960s.

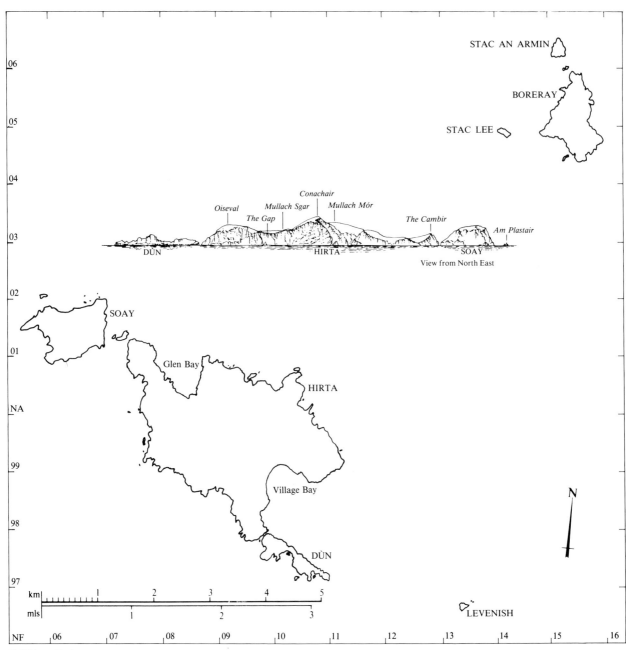

STAC AN ARMIN

BORERAY

STAC LEE

Oiseval   *Conachair*
  The Gap *Mullach Sgar* *Mullach Mór*
                                      The Cambir   *Am Plastair*
DÙN   HIRTA   SOAY
                                  View from North East

06

05

04

03

02

SOAY

01   Glen Bay

NA   HIRTA

99

Village Bay

98

N

97   DÙN

km   1   2   3   4   5
mls   1   2   3

LEVENISH

NF   06   07   08   09   10   11   12   13   14   15   16

St Kilda archipelago

INTRODUCTION:
SETTLEMENT AND BUILDINGS

HISTORICAL EVIDENCE

In their Ninth Report to the Crown, issued in 1927 and published in the following year as a Preface to the *Inventory of Monuments in the Outer Hebrides and Skye*, the Commissioners of the Royal Commission on Ancient Monuments made a special acknowledgement: 'For their knowledge of the remains upon St Kilda your Commissioners are indebted to the kindness of Captain Patrick Grant, late of the Indian Army, who happened to be visiting the island'.[1] This is one indication of the difficulties of access which this remote archipelago has always posed, lying as it does some sixty-four kilometres W of the Uists and Harris across the fearsome swell of the North Atlantic.

The record that was made by courtesy of Captain Grant comprised a single entry[2] relating to the earth-house or

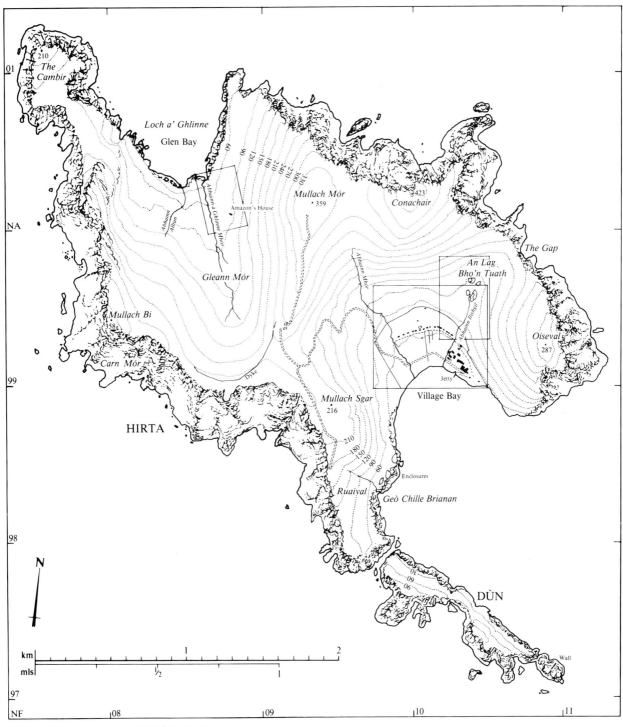

Hirta and Dùn; physical features and outlying structures

1

souterrain (No. **23**) in the village on Hirta, which had been examined by John Sands in 1876. Sands's account was also used as the basis for a brief note on other structures: most notably a bothy on the slopes of Mullach Sgar; a building in Gleann Mór on the N side of Hirta, known as the Amazon's House; a stretch of walling, assumed to be defensive, near the SE tip of the island of Dùn; an alleged stone circle on Boreray, first reported by the Reverend Kenneth Macaulay in 1758; and the 'House of the Staller', no longer extant, also on Boreray. The entry in the *Inventory* is dated July 1924, and at that date, six years prior to evacuation, there would have been little question of considering other buildings on the islands as ancient or historical monuments. The study of vernacular buildings and modern ethnology had not yet come of age.

The St Kildans themselves, however, had long been objects of tourist and antiquarian curiosity. First described briefly in 1549 by Dean Monro,[3] evidently through information provided by MacLeod of Harris's steward, St Kilda and the islanders' distinctive ways of life drew a succession of intrepid travellers, the earliest full-length, first-hand account being that by Martin Martin in 1697.[4] All descriptions dating from before the second quarter of the 19th century are especially valuable, however, for it was during the incumbency of the Reverend Neil Mackenzie (1829–43), the first resident minister for a century, that great changes took place in the character of the village settlement. At that period it began to assume its familiar crescentic layout with a street and associated cultivation plots formed within a head dyke. Fortunately, the earliest known view of the village shows the settlement prior to the reorganisation of the 1830s, its general shape and setting corresponding to what can be gleaned from early descriptions and maps. The view, one of a pair dating from 1812 was drawn by Sir Thomas Dyke Acland, a Devon man who in 1834 left £20 with the minister 'in order to encourage the people to build better houses'.[5]

Martin observed that 'the inhabitants live together in a small village . . . seated in a valley surrounded with four mountains serving as ramparts of defence. . . . There is a very large well near the town called St Kilder's Well'.[6] Near-contemporary information collected by Sir Robert Sibbald added that one of the three chapels on Hirta was

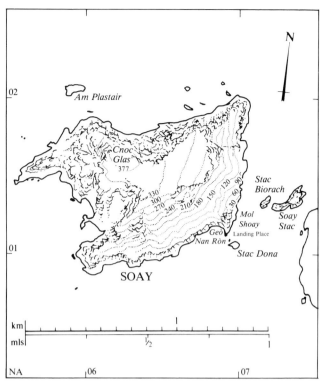

A   Soay; physical features

'close upon the town', and described the village as a 'small town . . . divided into four orderly streets, the largest of which they call the High Street'.[7] Macaulay maintained the urban likeness: '. . . at the distance of a quarter of a mile from the bay . . . the whole body of this little people live[s] together, like the inhabitants of a town or city. All their houses are built in two rows, abundantly regular and facing one another, with a tolerable causeway in the middle, which they call the street'.[8]

Estimates of the numbers of houses varied. There were about twenty-seven families in Martin's time and a century later, in 1799, twenty-six houses were in use.[9]* In arriving

B   Village and bay; view from S by Sir Thomas Dyke Acland, 1812

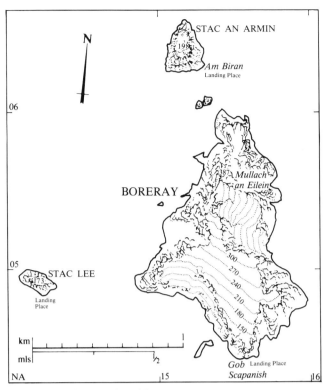

A *Boreray and the Stacs; physical features*

at this figure, Lord Brougham was assisted by his
companion, Robert Campbell, who produced the first
reasonably accurate map of St Kilda. At the time of
Mackenzie's reorganisation there were probably about
thirty occupied houses, although, as he recognised, some
were more ancient than others. According to his account,
'when new houses were built . . . afterwards, all these,

except one small one in which dwelt a widow, were
removed'.[10]

The processes of renewal produced a variety in
appearance and construction that was noted by early
commentators. Acland's drawing of the 'Principal Square
in the Capital of St Kilda' in 1812 shows buildings with
straw-thatched roofs carried on both the inner and the
outer edges of the walls. The latter type was observed in
1819 by MacCulloch who decried it as being 'in the
barbarous manner practised in Skye, in Barra, and in other
places'.[11] Mackenzie, on the other hand, drew attention to
the thick double walls that contained bed recesses and
supported rafters on their inner edges; externally, 'as most
of the houses touched each other, there was thus left from
house to house a broad grassy walk on the top of the
walls'.[12]

Martin described the houses as being 'of a low form, and
the doors all to the north-east to secure them from the
shocks of the tempestuous south-west winds. The walls of
the houses are rudely built of stone, the short couples
joining at the ends of the roof, upon whose sides small ribs
of wood are laid, and these covered with straw; the whole
secured by ropes made of twisted heath, the extremity of
which on each side is poised with stone to preserve the
thatch from being blown away'.[13] According to Macaulay,
however, the drystone walls were by no means low; their
height of between 8 and 9 ft (2·4 m–2·7 m) was unusually
high for the Western Isles, and allowed the St Kildans to
accumulate manure within their houses over winter to a
depth of about 4 ft (1·2 m) which they then put on their
spring sowing of barley. 'All their dwelling houses',
Macaulay continued, 'are divided into two apartments by
partition walls. In the division next the door, which is much
the largest, they have their cattle stored during the whole
winter season; the other serves for kitchen, hall and
bedroom. . . In the heart of the walls are the beds, which
are overlaid with flags, and large enough to contain three
persons. In the side of every bed is an opening by way of a

B *Houses in the 'Principal Square in the Capital of St Kilda';
view by Sir Thomas Dyke Acland, 1812*

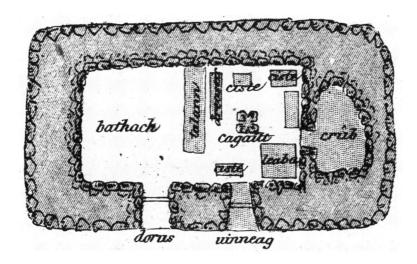

'Taigh Dubh with Crub'
(Black house with wall-bed);
plan published 1870

door, which is much too narrow and low to answer that purpose'.[14] A later 18th-century visitor likened them to stone-vaulted ovens, disposed around the walls of their huts according to the size of the family.[15]

The most graphic description of a domestic interior with wall-beds was provided by Mackenzie who reckoned that 'at times a visit to a parishioner was quite an adventure. . . Inside the door you had to climb over the manure . . . among the cattle, which, on account of the presence of a stranger, and the barking of dogs, and the shouting of your friends above, soon got very excited. Amidst great confusion and excitement you got helped along and over the dividing *fallan* [partition]. Here you had to creep along on hands and feet, as it was only near the centre of the space that you could even sit upright. Carefully creeping along in the almost total darkness, you made your way to the top of the steep slope which led down to the bed opening. Down this you went head foremost, nothing visible above but your legs, while you spoke and prayed'.[16]

These were the houses that Mackenzie sought to replace after 1834, using Acland's gift to purchase luxuries such as beds and windows. The unwholesome practice of internal manure accumulation was discouraged by the provision of specially designated manure houses and pits outside. Mackenzie intended to make the houses larger, but building size was limited by lack of roofing timber. Only old timber and driftwood was available, and despite the acquisition of a saw and the creation of a sawpit to cut up driftwood, 'it was not very often that a log fit for use was secured, as owing to the rocky nature of the shore and constant surf, it was generally ground to matchwood'.[17]

Macaulay recorded that all the arable land in the village was 'divided out into a great many unequal plots and every one of these is in a manner enclosed and kept invariably within the same bounds'.[18] Each plot was sufficiently distinctive to be 'discriminated from all the rest; the whole body of the people may in a stormy day assemble together in one place, and without any difficulty divide all their ground at a fire-side, without perambulating or taking a survey of it . . .'.[19] In 1834 the villagers agreed to have the land reallocated among them 'so that each might build upon his own portion'.[20] Unhappy with the results of arbitration, they divided the land themselves, making the divisions as equal as possible, and apportioned them by lot. After the houses were built, the arable ground was cleared of stones, drained and enclosed by a head dyke and a high seaward wall for protecting seeds and crops. In order to encourage the others, the minister himself had to take a personal lead in almost all of the physical work.

The effects of Mackenzie's architectural and agrarian reorganisation are graphically displayed in a plan of the village by Sharbau, a draughtsman who carried out a survey in July 1858 and added details in 1860 and 1861.[21]*

The boundaries are represented in schematic form, and most of the numerous storehouses within the head dyke are omitted, but otherwise the drawing is reliable and pays close attention to detail. This plan has enabled modern fieldworkers on St Kilda to understand structural complexities, and to give meaning to otherwise unintelligible building foundations, and within the immediate vicinity of the street to establish that what is not shown on the drawing was not actually there at the date of survey. The plan also denotes the designated functions of ancillary buildings for storing corn, fish, birds and manure, and the uses of enclosed yards for cabbages and potatoes.

Reference is made to the occurrence of at least two wall-beds, so despite Mackenzie's good intentions, old cosy habits died hard. The holders of the plots on either side of the street are named, and the names and divisions of the outer and inner crofts correspond, except in the centre of the village, thus making eighteen outer and nineteen inner strips; Betty Scott's Cottage (Black House K, No. **8**), which Captain Thomas surveyed in detail, was associated with one of the central strips.[22] Three pairs of crofts were marked as common ground because their former occupants had 'gone to Australia', a touching reminder of the emigration in 1856 of thirty-six islanders, half of whom died on voyage or in quarantine.[23] The broad eastern strip of common ground, now largely occupied by the army camp, probably represented three original divisions, making a total of twenty-one or twenty-two houses and associated cultivation plots.

In October 1860 a hurricane swept away the thatched roofs of many of the black houses, and during the summer of 1861 work began on the first of a series of sixteen cottages under the direction of craftsmen from the Dunvegan estate.[24] Two new houses are marked on Sharbau's plan, and these (Houses 5 and 9) constitute the beginnings of a second housing revolution in the 19th-century village.

The era of photography on St Kilda also began in about 1860, and photographs taken in the following decades provide an accurate visual record of the St Kildan community and its buildings. Although poignantly charting the process of physical decline, these photographs show, among other things, surprising evidence of removals and reconstructions of the cleitean within and around the head dyke.[25]

Photographs taken in 1886 and 1986 from the steep slope of Oiseval, E of the village, demonstrate some of the changes that took place over a century. Apart from the obvious intrusion of the Ministry of Defence establishment with its associated road and quarry, there is the jetty, built in 1901. Several cleitean on the lower meadows and Cleit 1 just above the Store (No. **1**) have appeared since 1886, whilst a cleit below the Factor's House has been demol-

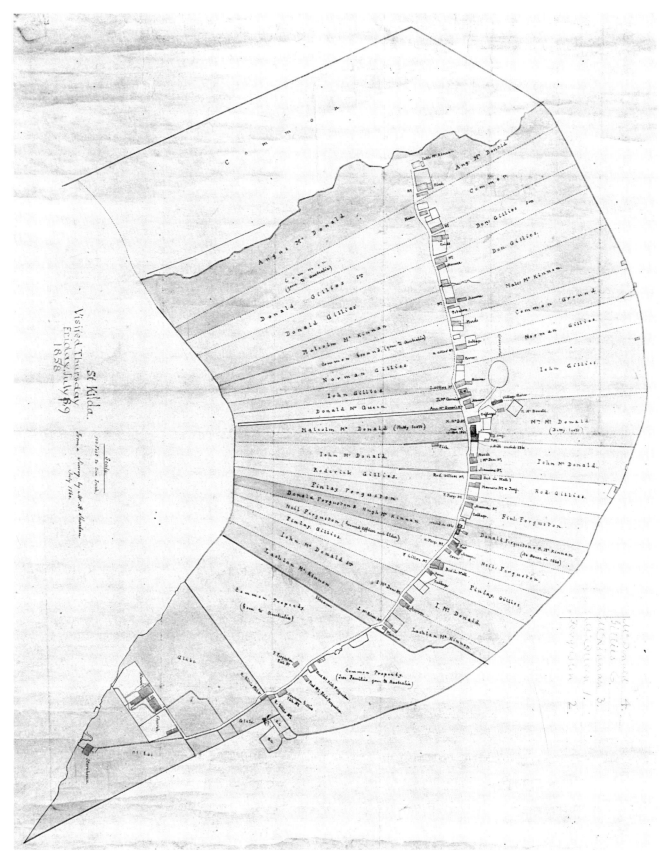

Village; survey by Sharbau, 1858 and 1860 (see also detail on cover)

5

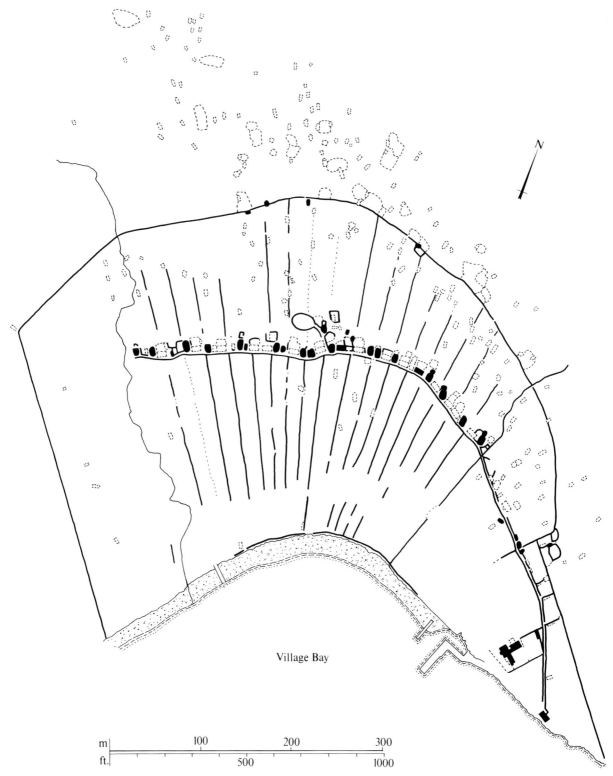

Village Bay

Village; distribution plan of remains identifiable from Sharbau survey

ished and another (12) built a little further down the slope. The photograph of 1886 shows domed roofs of thatch on the black houses between the newer houses, and there is clear evidence of cultivation in places, particularly below the Factor's House. In photographs taken from the foot of Conachair, a similar range of contrasts can be observed. In the left foreground, for instance, the Bull's House (No. **3**) is thatched, and to the right of it is an enclosure which has since been largely removed, most of the stone having gone into the building of a cleit. The cell at the N end of Cleit 137 (No. **19**), visible in the foreground of the photograph of

1986, appears to have been whole and roofed in 1886, and there have been alterations to the enclosure to its right. Just to the left of the burial-ground an enclosure present in 1886 has almost disappeared, most of the stone probably having been used in the erection of Cleit 80.

Photographs taken from a spot W of the burial-ground in 1886, 1930 and 1986 show additional details of some houses: in the earliest view almost all visible black houses are thatched and hip-roofed, although Black House Z appears to be roofless. In the nearer houses skylights lighting the inner middle rooms can be seen clearly. In 1930

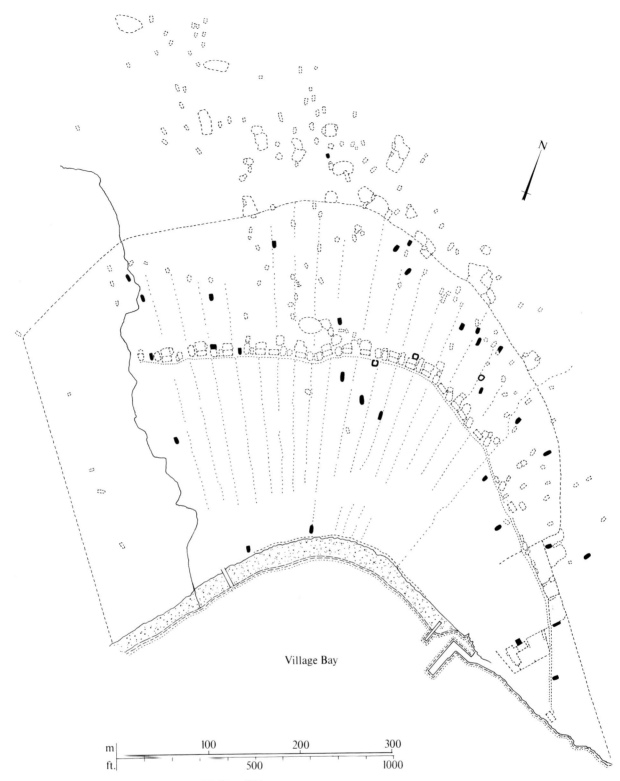

Village; distribution plan of buildings built or remodelled since 1886

Black House L (No. **9**) was still thatched, as was M, with the addition of a form of tarpaulin, but N seems to have been roofless and O had acquired gables and a tarred felt roof (No. **10**). Further along the street Black House B has a hipped roof, but A has gables and felt covering. None of the black houses in the area of the Factor's House is roofed, but several changes are evident among the cleitean in that area and in the glebe; there is also a new cleit on the slope above the head dyke. On the evidence of photographs taken in 1886 a number of cleitean have been newly built or remodelled usually involving an increase in length or

height, or a change in the position of the doorway. Some cleitean disappeared altogether between 1886 and 1930.

Two other photographs were taken slightly earlier, possibly in 1878, for Valentines of Dundee. Comparison can be made between one of these and one taken in 1986 from almost the same position. In the earlier view the School (No. **2**) is absent; the small building at the lower end of Black House W (No. **11**) is thatched, as is Black House Z, but Black House X, thatched in 1886, was evidently roofless. The modern photograph shows that Cleitean 24, 27 and 29 have been remodelled and that 25 has been

A

B

Village; A   general view from E, 1886
B   view from E, c. 1878

A

B

Village: A, B   views from E

A

B

Village; A   general view from N, 1886
B   E end; view from NW, c. 1878

A

B

Village: A   general view from N
B   House 5 and Post Office from SE, 1930

A

B

Village, 1938; A   Houses 2–6 from SE (with Finlay MacQueen)
B   House 10 and Black House M, from E

A

Village; A high-level view from N, 1938
        B   Black House B; window, 1938
        C   House 5; interior, 1949
            (including framework of loom and
            a quern-stone)

B

rebuilt in a slightly different position. In another pair of
contrasting views the earlier photograph shows that Cleit
32 (No. **12**) was thatched and that the walling over the
doorway was noticeably neater. All the visible black houses
had thatched and hipped roofs. The enclosure where Cleit
80 now stands, just in front of the burial-ground, shows
clearly, and there are several alterations affecting cleitean.

Alastair Alpin MacGregor's photographs taken in
August 1930 record the state of the buildings when the
islanders were preparing to evacuate their homes. In one
view House 4 is only half-roofed, the main portion of Black
House F is roofless although the northern building is
thatched, and all other visible black houses (C, D, E, G and
H) have added gables and felt-covered roofs. There is a
rotary quernstone lying at the foot of the gable of Black
House E (No. **6**).

Even after the evacuation of the last thirty-six persons in
August 1930, however, some houses continued to be maintained by those who returned to their island homes
in the following summers. Robert Atkinson made a
memorable photographic record of one such revisit in 1938
when he joined Finlay MacQueen, Mrs Gillies, and her son
Neil, who was employed as a bird-watcher by the new
owner, Lord Dumfries, later 5th Marquis of Bute.[26] Their
houses (2 and 11) and the Fergusons' (House 5) were still
cared for, but the view through Atkinson's camera was
generally one of unremitting decay, providing a sad but
useful record of the carpentry and fittings associated with
the latest phases of domestic habitation.

Maps and drawings continued to supplement the information from photographs, but there is irony in the fact that
the St Kilda group of islands only became fully recorded
almost at the point of their desertion, the first Ordnance
Survey map being published in 1928.[27]

C

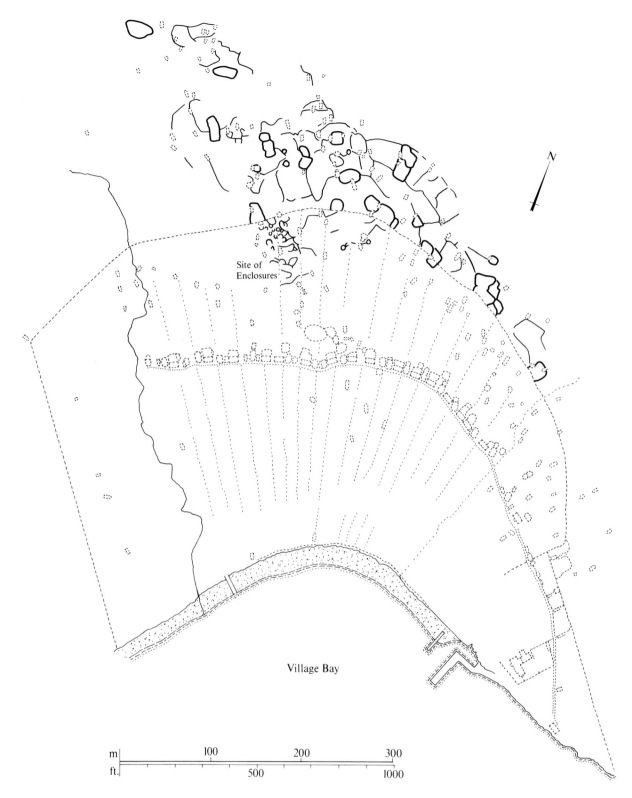

Site of
Enclosures

N

Village Bay

m | 100   200   300
ft. | 500   1000

Village; distribution plan of outlying enclosures and dykes

A

B

Village from N; A high-level view
B area of early settlement

EVIDENCE OF FIELD SURVEY

As is well known, Hirta was re-occupied in 1957 for
military use as a tracking station for a missile range in the
Uists. The detachment was housed first in temporary
Nissen huts and, after 1966, in more permanent
accommodation in the E sector of Village Bay.[28] Whilst
causing attention to be focussed sharply on environmental
and conservation matters, this permanent military presence
provided opportunities that were hitherto beyond practical
reach. Since assuming ownership of the islands in 1956/7,
for instance, the National Trust for Scotland has
consolidated and restored a number of buildings in the
village, and the seasonal accommodation provided by these
buildings has enabled surveys of all kinds to be carried out.

The most recent in a series of surveys of antiquities and
field monuments[29] was that undertaken by the Royal
Commission on the Ancient and Historical Monuments of
Scotland in 1983–6. This survey covered three large areas
of settlement on Hirta: the Village, An Lag, and Gleann
Mór, as well as providing detailed treatment of individual
buildings within those areas.

i VILLAGE: THE SETTLEMENT. Outside the areas
affected by successive army encampments, the boundaries
of the cultivation strips recorded by Sharbau remain
reasonably clearly defined, especially by the central consumption dykes. Those crofts associated with Houses 12,
13 and 16 and marked as common ground on Sharbau's
plan contain complex patterns of subdivided cultivation
formed in terraces and strips. The upper part of the former
common ground E of Abhainn Ilishgil (the Dry Burn),
originally associated with perhaps three houses, exhibits a
similar pattern, which is traceable on aerial photographs.

Mackenzie's impressive head dyke is more complicated
than appears at first sight; parts of it are built in dis-
continuous stretches and at many points, particularly in the
centre, it abuts earlier cleit-like structures and enclosures.
Gateways in the dyke gave access from many of the
divisions to the hillside beyond but some gaps have been
blocked by later walling.

Enclosures within the area of the head dyke include the
gardens at the back of the dwelling-houses, a few small
circular and gateless yards akin to the 'plantiecrues' of the
Northern Isles,[30] and the oval burial-ground in the centre of
the village. There is a greater number of enclosures outside
the head dyke, especially in the stony lower slopes of
Conachair around Tobar Childa. Their positions and
irregularities of form bring to mind Macaulay's comment
about 'unequal plots' and defy ready explanation, but some
show faint traces of ridging and terracing, indicating a
former use for sheltering crops. Foundations of similar
enclosures are still visible within the area of the head dyke,
and it may be presumed that a pattern similar to that

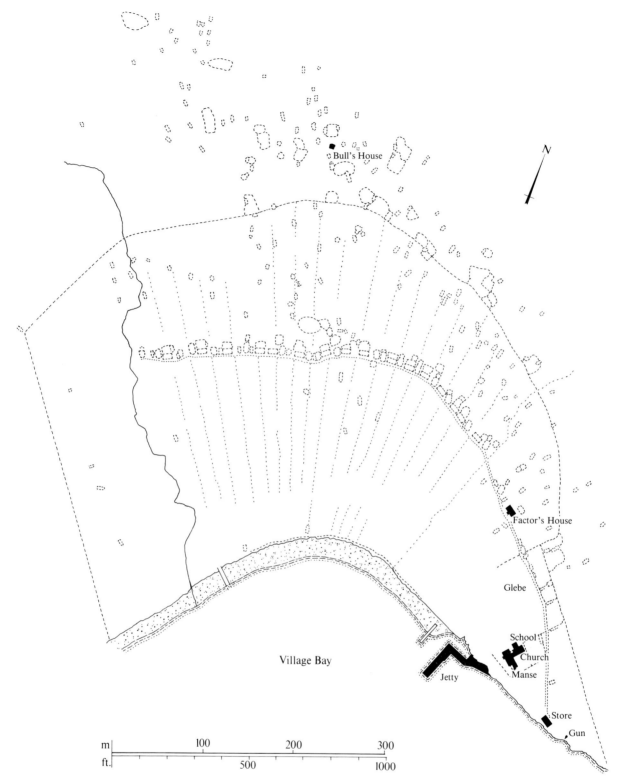

N

Bull's House

Factor's House

Glebe

School
Church
Manse

Village Bay

Jetty

Store

Gun

m		100		200		300
ft.			500			1000

Village; distribution plan of estate and community buildings

outside existed throughout much of the early village before the 1830s.

Surviving remains of the 'streets' associated with the early village run mainly across the NE sector of the site. They appear as stretches of grassy terracing, scarped and partly revetted, in some cases overlain by later cleitean or enclosures. The best-preserved section, which lies within the head dyke and is traceable from a point on the hillside N of the Factor's House, is blocked in this way, and is flanked by at least one building of early type (Cleit 32; No. **12**).

Each of the crofts has at least one cleit, usually situated above the street, but these structures have a noticeably E and central distribution-pattern, the dampish area towards the Abhainn Mhór being relatively blank.

One anomalous feature in the lower meadow is a subterranean stone-lined cell or chamber (No. **24**), which is covered with a slab, apparently similar to one discovered by Mackenzie when he was clearing land for the glebe. He also described how 'the stones removed from the land in the course of these operations were built into a thick wall around the little field, but after removing most there remained two stones which were too heavy to remove, and as they were lying flat and occupying a good deal of space I raised them up on end. They may puzzle some future antiquary'.[31]

ii VILLAGE: ESTATE AND COMMUNITY BUILDINGS. These buildings are grouped in the SE quarter of Village Bay close to the traditional landing-place on the rocks below. An attempt was made in the early 1860s to blast out a more sheltered landing in this area but the work remained incomplete, and the existing slipway and concrete jetty were not built until 1901.

The two-storeyed and gabled building (No. **1**) closest to the shoreline was erected by the estate some time before 1819[32]* to store the commodities that were gathered by the villagers in payment of their rent in kind, namely, tweed, oil, fish and feathers. It was thus the first of the storeyed buildings on the island. The roof and E half of the front wall were damaged by gunfire from a German U-boat which entered Village Bay in May 1918 with the aim of destroying the island's wireless transmitter. In October 1918, wise after the event, the Admiralty installed a naval gun and ammunition-store nearby, and in 1986 the store

itself was repaired and re-roofed to provide additional bothy accommodation.

The building where the factor stayed during his annual visits to collect the rent stands towards the lower end of the street, close to the church and manse. Built on common ground, probably in the later 1860s, it is of a conventional mainland type with one and a half storeys and a projecting front porch.

The church (No. **2**), a relatively plain two-bay oblong structure, was built in accordance with plans prepared by Robert Stevenson in 1826.[33]* A view dating from Acland's visit in 1834 shows church and manse, linked by a walled passage, occupying what was then a somewhat isolated situation.[34] A schoolroom was added on the NW side in 1900 and, following years of neglect after the evacuation, the church and school were restored, and the church re-dedicated in 1980. The buildings now stand within the precincts of the military camp and the manse serves as the Sergeants' Mess, but some impressive stretches of the manse garden and glebe walls, laid out by the indefatigable Mackenzie, still survive around and above the E end of the street.

Prior to the 1820s, visiting or resident ministers had enjoyed no special domestic or liturgical facilities. By the early 19th century the three chapels described by Martin Martin – Christ Church or Chapel, St Brianan's (Brendan's), and St Columba's – were little more than a memory, although one visitor in 1815 claimed that 'very obscure traces of two still remain'.[35] According to Martin, Christ Chapel was the largest, 'near the village . . . covered and thatched after the manner of their houses'.[36] Macaulay added that 'it was built of stone and without any cement: its length is 24 feet [7·32 m], and its breadth 14 [4·27 m]. This was in former times the principle (*sic*) place of worship in the isle, and here they continue to bury their dead'.[37] Its churchyard was the most likely source of the grooved crosses of Early Christian type built into the front wall of House 16 and into the slabbed roof of Cleit 74,[38] which is situated a short distance W of the present oval burial-ground. This burial-ground, almost certainly the site of Christ Church itself, is set within an impressive battered wall, and to Mackenzie this 'was the portion of our work in which I took the greatest personal interest, as there I buried three of my children who died in infancy'.[39] A headstone in

17

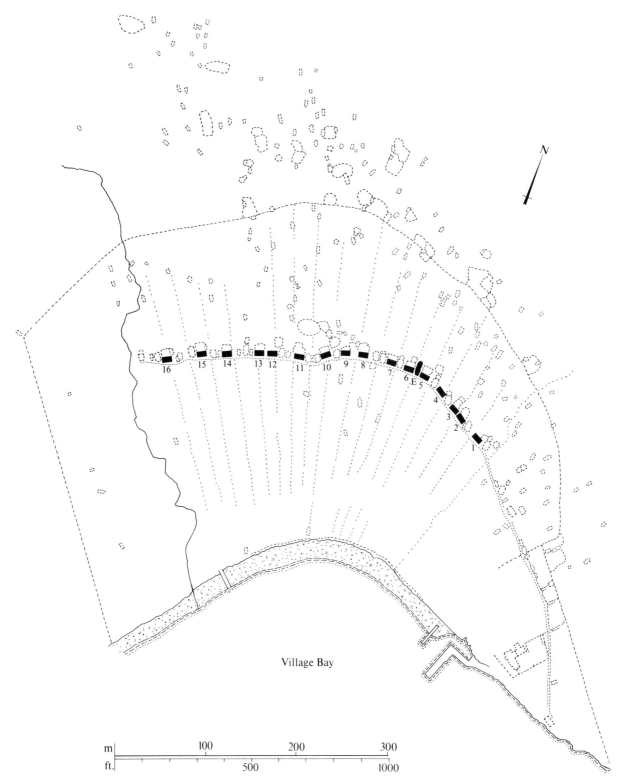

Village Bay

m		100		200		300
ft.			500			1000

Village; distribution plan of houses dating from 1861 and later

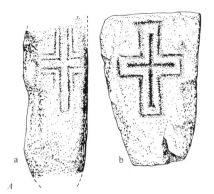

A   Cross-marked stones a *from House 16 and* b *from Cleit 74, Village*
B   Burial-ground from NW   C   in 1930

the burial-ground commemorates these three Mackenzie infants.

Two other buildings for communal use are marked on Sharbau's plan. Whether the structure described as a 'mill erected in 1861' was in fact a grain-mill and had a working existence is not known, but the alignment and jointing of walling and the nature of some of the openings around Black Houses I and J are certainly unusual, quite unlike anything else in the village. On the other hand, the use of quernstones for milling, mainly by the womenfolk, is well attested later in the 19th century, and, if water power had been involved, there is no clear indication of a water-course in this area. Also marked as an overlay on Sharbau's plan is the 'village barn', and Black House L (No. **9**) appears to be a modified and truncated version of this structure with exposed foundations at the N end.

It is possible that the building previously known as 'medieval house T'[40], here Black House W (No. **11**), had a related function. To Williamson and Boyd this small thick-walled building 'stands on the site of a much larger, ovate-oblong structure reminiscent of a Viking house-type'.[41] There appears, however, to be no corroboration of this. The small gabled building at the lower (south-western) end is probably not of any antiquity, while part of the larger structure, which stood some distance from the houses, might plausibly be identified as a kiln or kiln-barn. The slightly raised platform at the rounded end possibly contained the kiln-bowl, and although unusually set at the uphill end of a sloping site, its general outline bears a superficial resemblance to other Hebridean kilns.[42] The rebuilt lower portion contains a drain and traces of a possible winnowing-passage.

Martin mentions that 'they have only one common kiln which serves them all by turns, as the lots fall to their share . . .'[43] One visitor in 1841 described 'a visit to the national kiln, in which the people . . . dry their corn. It consisted of two dark apartments, one within and of considerably higher level than the other, and a hole runs from a corner of the lower floor under that of the upper, in which a man sits to tend the fire. The grain is dried in the sheaf, and then threshed out on the lower floor'.[44] By 1858–60, although the village barn mentioned above still survived, the kiln appears to have gone out of use and was no longer remembered.

iii   VILLAGE: 19TH-CENTURY HOUSES. The six-teen houses erected in and after 1861 were lime-mortared, gabled and chimneyed. Of a standard mainland three-roomed design, these buildings are quite different from their predecessors; they face seaward, not end-on to the bay, and have a hard rectangular outline of mortared stone and chimneyed gables. Their roofs were covered with zinc plates nailed down to sarking boards as a security against the wind, but some plates were too short to cover the whole roof, and all were apparently prone to condensation; of them it was said that 'it rained inside whenever it rained outside'.[45] The zinc was subsequently replaced by tarred felt held down by spikes and stays, and that is how five of them have been re-roofed by the National Trust for Scotland. In 1898 they were provided with new floors which were partly of concrete, partly wooden. Set in to the slope, like the storehouse, most of these houses have a revetted drainage-ditch at the rear, a common mainland technique.

The construction of these houses caused modifications to

A

B

C

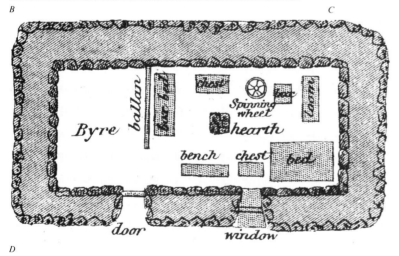

D

Village; A   Houses 5–8 and black houses from SE
B   Black Houses P and Q, from E
C   Black House R; W side-wall,
    detail of wall-plate
D   'Betty Scott's Cottage'
    (Black House K);
    plan published 1870

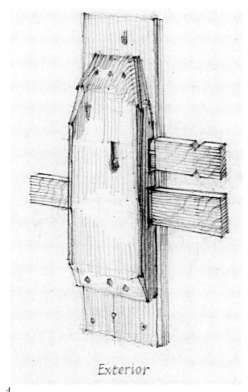

Exterior

A

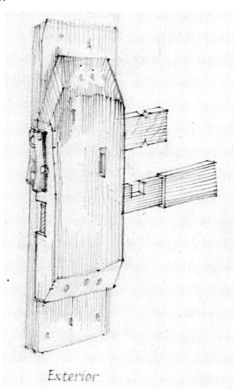

Exterior

B

A, B Wooden tumbler-lock
      (from St Kilda, now in Highland Folk Museum, Kingussie);
      sketches by G D Hay, 1975

the building pattern on the street frontage, but most new structures appear to have been fitted into the gaps between the black houses, many of which were relegated to use as byres and stores. However, on Sharbau's plan one new house is shown partly overlying an older structure, and immediately E of House 8 (No. **4**) there are the foundations of a black house partly overlaid by its successor, its removal having left a gap in front of the W doorway of Black House H.[46]

It is also evident that a number of single persons of lowly status in the St Kildan hierarchy retained unimproved dwellings. Such was the case with the spinster, Rachel MacCrimmon, whose house is identifiable as Black House X.[47] It stands in the area of common ground at the E end of the village and had evidently been taken over from one of the emigrant families.

Close examination of Sharbau's plan shows that at least one of the round-angled black houses post-dates 1860. Black House E (No. **6**), evidently the last of its kind to be built on St Kilda, appears to have been gable-ended from the outset, but otherwise it conforms to the traditional layout. With tethering rings on the inner wall-face and a drain under the centre of the gable-wall, the neatly built lower end obviously served as a byre.

The black houses of the 1830s were at first hip-roofed, and their stepped profiles show how secondary gables have been superimposed on original broad wall-heads. Black House G (No. **7**) is a typical specimen, with a byre and a window-lit dwelling at the lower and upper ends respectively. The straight joints at the corners of the N end-wall appear to indicate a refacing. The outer face of this wall recently collapsed, revealing the remains of what was probably an access passage to a wall-bed which had been removed upon the construction of the N annexe.

There are at least six black houses in which the N end-wall appears to have been refaced in this manner. External irregularities in wall alignments also suggest that some of these buildings have been remodelled out of older structures. Black House K (No. **8**), for example, which is situated in the vicinity of the old village, is of much less regular outline than that shown in Captain Thomas's drawing of 1860, where, named Betty Scott's Cottage, it appears complete with its domestic plenishings.[48]

Few fixtures and fittings survive *in situ*, but many items have found their way into museums and displays. One well-known feature was the use of wooden locks and keys, but sliding wooden tumbler-locks, which had a tendency to swell when damp, were not so peculiar to St Kilda as was once thought, even though six, possibly seven, out of twenty-two known Scottish examples are from Hirta.[49] They certainly kept inquisitive visitors at bay, T S Muir recording that 'the people being assembled in church, we found the doors in most instances secured by a large wooden lock, so ingeniously contrived that we were utterly unable so much as to conjecture by what means it could be opened. The thing, made up of a square of several sturdy bars immovably jammed ends and sides together, and without a catch or key-hole, was certainly a puzzle that would have honoured a Chubb or a Chinaman.'[50]

iv VILLAGE: EARLY HOUSES AND STRUCTURES. At least a dozen cleit-like buildings in the backlands of the village represent modifications of older structures, which correspond generally with what is known from historical sources of prevailing house-types before the 1830s. Most have been rebuilt, re-aligned or heightened to serve as cleitean, but the ancestry of an outlying structure such as Cleit 122/3 (No. **18**) is clearly evident from its plan and from the nature of the adjacent beehive cell, obviously a former sleeping chamber linked by a narrow lintelled passage. Similarly, Cleit 137 (No. **19**) is of a larger and broader oblong plan than normal, and retains clear vestiges

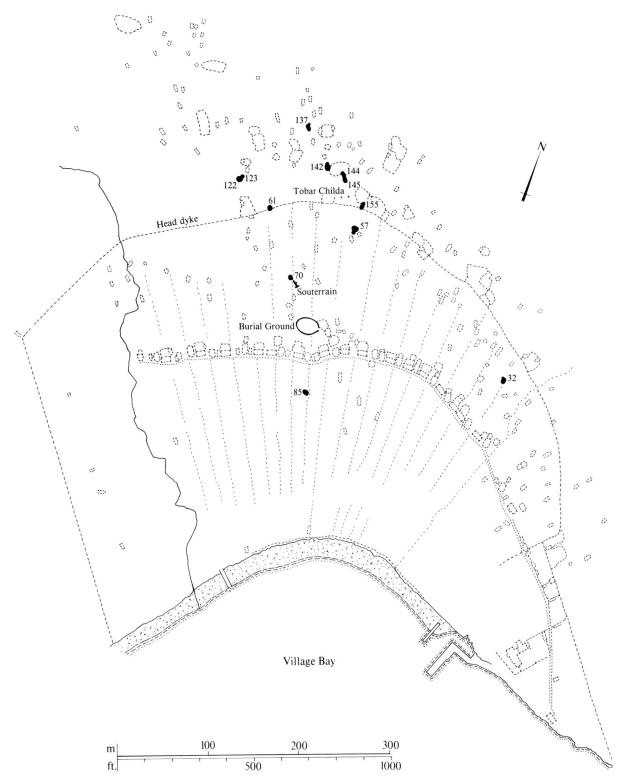

137

142 144

122 123 Tobar Childa

145

61 155

Head dyke 57

70

Souterrain

Burial Ground

32

85

Village Bay

m	100	200	300
ft.	500	1000	

Village; distribution plan of early structures

of a cell and linking passage at the N angle. It shows
evidence of reconstruction, as does its near-neighbour,
Cleit 142 (No. **20**). In the narrower conjoined Cleit 144–5
(No. **21**), the upper chamber has been enlarged out of a
small cell and part of the linking passage still survives.

Within the head dyke, Cleit 32 (No. **12**), which stands on
the edge of an early terrace-way, is of roughly oval plan,
and has been altered and repaired at the upper and lower
ends, latterly having had a wooden roof-structure covered
with roped thatch. Remains of openings to one, possibly
two, cell annexes betray an earlier origin. Also within the
head dyke is Calum Mór's House (Cleit 57; No. **13**) which
is reputed to have been built by a legendary strong man in a
day. However, the name is of relatively recent application,
suggesting perhaps that for a long time it was merely one of
several old houses. The turf covering has been renewed but
otherwise the structure remains much as built, a semi-
subterranean, windowless building with massive corbelled
blocks forming a continuous wall and roof. Inside, there
are blocked entries to two annexes, the circular foundations
of one cell remaining clearly visible outside. Overall, the
building conforms well to Mackenzie's description of the
most ancient houses in the 1830s: '. . . the walls are not
perched, but contracted gradually by the overlapping of the
stones to nearly a point. The entrance door is about three
feet by two and a half feet [0·91 m by 0·76 m]. The outside is
covered with earth and rubbish and appears like a green
hillock.'[51]

Cleit 85 (No. **17**), which lies below the W half of the
street, purports to be a reconstruction of the house where
Rachel Chiesly, Lady Grange, spent about eight years in
exile after being banished to St Kilda by her husband, the
Lord Justice Clerk, in 1734. Although an unusually large
cleit of irregular plan and bearing traces of older work, the
grounds for identifying this as her residence are dubious; in
any case, Sands on his visit in 1876 described her house as
having been demolished 'a few years ago'.[52]*

Many of these structures are pointers to old building
traditions, comparable in some respects to the cellular
forms of Early Historic origin excavated on North Uist and
in Orkney.[53] But these St Kilda buildings cannot be readily
dated without the aid of archaeological excavation. They
are certainly pre-1830, and Cleit 57, Calum Mór's House,
is of a type that Mackenzie considered to be comparatively

speaking 'most ancient'. But how ancient is 'ancient' in this
context?

The only structure in the village that has been occasion-
ally, though incompletely, excavated is the souterrain
(No. **23**), which lies to the NW of the burial-ground.
Known to the St Kildans as the 'House of the Fairies', the
souterrain consists of a lintelled passage, over 10 m long,
with at least one lateral branch. The true inner or NW end
has not been located, but the passage is obviously heading
in the direction of the mound beneath a later dyke and
Cleit 70, an atypical cleit. Its relationship to these above-
ground features and its date require further clarification.
Since its discovery in 1844 the souterrain has been
excavated on at least four occasions, most recently in
1974.[54] Finds from the site may demonstrate a period of use
in either the first or early second millennium AD.

v AN LAG BHO 'N TUATH. An Lag, the corrie-like
hollow NE of the village, nestling between Conachair and
Oiseval on the route to The Gap, is an area in which
structural remains have attracted the close attention of field
archaeologists in recent decades.[55]*

Some of the irregular enclosures within An Lag have
been extended and modified in their circuits. Although
generally interpreted as sheep stells, their walls, vertically-
faced externally and battered internally, appear to have
been constructed to exclude rather than contain livestock.
One enclosure overlies a tract of rig-like gravel mounds, the
natural effects of solifluction, but elsewhere there are
indications of cultivation affected by later turf cutting. An
Lag is a naturally sheltered arena, and these enclosures may
have arisen in an attempt, perhaps in the 1830s, to enclose
suitable land for growing vegetables.

Many of the standing cleitean are placed in lines on the
surrounding slopes of Conachair and The Gap. Some have
been re-erected on mounded foundations, and a group of
structures in the rocky outcrop at the foot of the route to
The Gap may have originated as a settlement, possibly a
house and enclosure. However, the twenty or so allegedly
boat-shaped settings, concentrated on the SW shoulder of
An Lag, present a particularly difficult problem. Their date
and purpose may only be elucidated by larger-scale excavation than has so far been undertaken. A sample of organic
material from one setting, recovered in 1973, yielded a

An Lag Bho 'n Tuath and The Gap from S

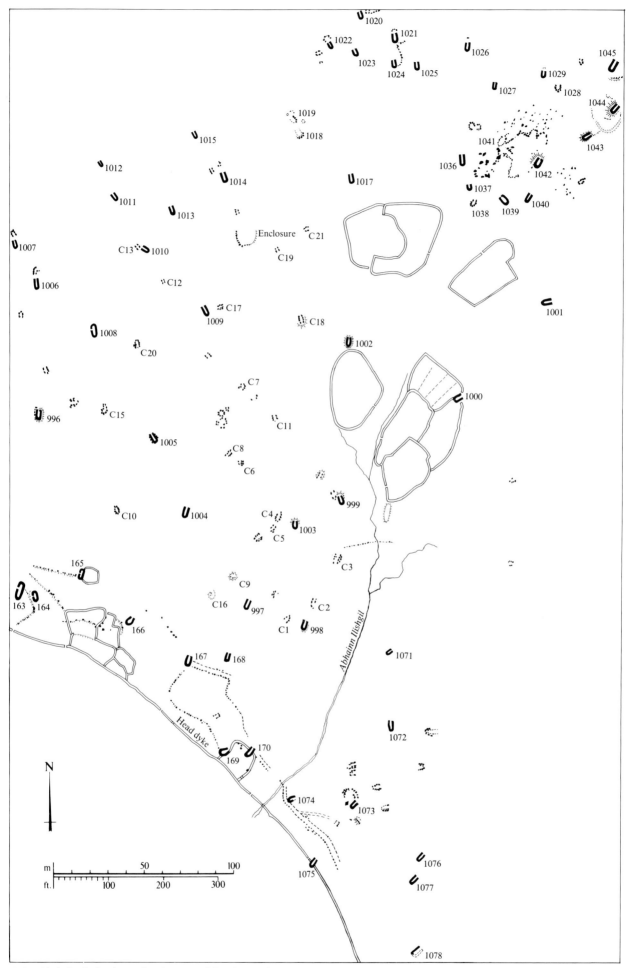

An Lag Bho 'n Tuath; distribution plan (for system of identification of structures, see p. ix)

A

An Lag Bho 'n Tuath: A   general view from NE
                       B   specimen 'boat-shaped' setting
                       C   plan of ?enclosure

radiocarbon determination of 1833 bc ±47 (SRR–316), but
the relationship of the dated material with the stone setting
is by no means certain.[56]

Ground survey has revealed no convincing 'prow' or
'stern' stones as might be expected in a boat-shaped setting
of Norse origin. Some of the structures in An Lag also have
stones placed parallel to, and outside, the 'boat-shaped'
outline, and these could represent the inner and outer wall-
faces of robbed cleitean. The settings are also similar in size
to cleitean; they are certainly man-made, and building
materials for the later and extensive enclosure-walls in An
Lag presumably came from somewhere close at hand.

B

vi   GLEANN MÓR: SETTLEMENT. In Gleann Mór,
on the N side of Hirta, evidence of settlement and land use
is concentrated in two main areas around the lower reaches
of the Abhainn a' Ghlinne Mhóir. Traces of lazy-beds in a
small patch further to the W probably relate to an episode
described by Macaulay: 'the steward . . . prevailed with
some of the people, a few years ago, to make an experiment
on two or three small spots there, by turning and sowing
them'.[57] The results were not good, and the St Kildans felt
that it was a waste of land better suited for pasture.
Macaulay himself also registered the belief that the ground
here 'is incomparably better in some parts of it than that
round the village'; he considered that 'the cattle . . . feed
most luxuriously during the summer season on the plots of
grass . . .; and here they yield, it may naturally be expected,
more than ordinary quantities of milk'.[58] The use of this
rich grazing for summer shieling persisted into modern
times, Mackenzie noting that 'here the cattle and sheep
were kept during the time when they might injure the crops
. . . on the other side of the island'.[59] He implied that the St

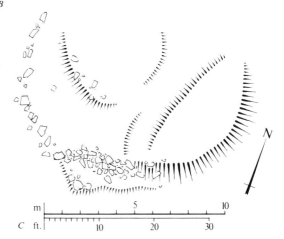

m   5   10
C   ft.   10   20   30

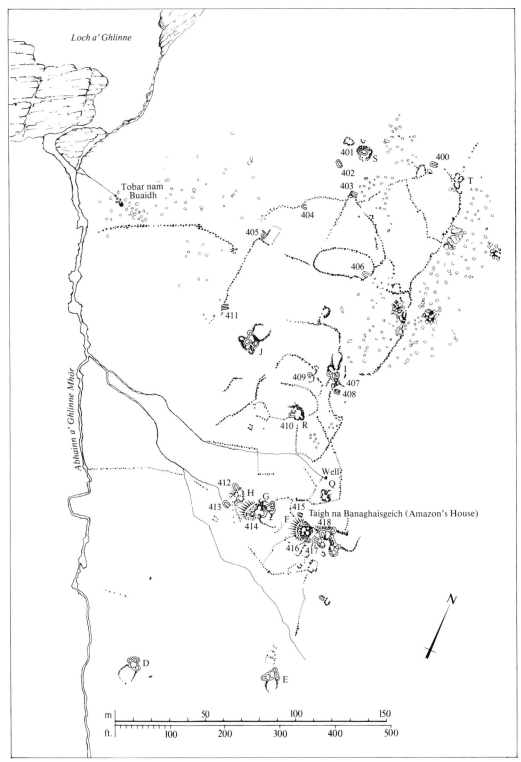

Loch a' Ghlinne

Tobar nam
Buaidh

Abhainn a' Ghlinne Mhòr

401 S
402
403
404
405
406
411
J
409 I
407
408
410 R
Well
Q
412 H G
413 415
414 F
416 417 418
Taigh na Banaghaisgeich (Amazon's House)
400
T

D
E

m		50		100		150
ft.	100	200	300	400	500	

N

Gleann Mòr, NE area

Kildan women travelled daily to milk cows and ewes, and photographic evidence of such practices was published in 1900.[60]

The densest cluster of buildings is on the E side of the burn where there is scree material available for building, a well-drained slope, and a water-supply from at least three springs, including Tobar nam Buaidh close to the shore. However, there is no reliable landing-place, nor is there historical record of permanent habitation. Such buildings as survive are known or are likely to have been used latterly for temporary or seasonal accommodation.

The buildings, including those of nucleated character such as the 'Amazon's House' (No. 26), occur in groups, and around them there is a complicated pattern of much-reduced dykes and enclosures comparable with those outside the head dyke in the village. Some dykes appear to emanate from, and are presumably coeval with, the buildings; others clearly abut the main structures and overlie the foundations of earlier buildings or dykes.

Around the head of the glen there is a long continuous turf dyke of unknown date and purpose, possibly originally intended as some form of territorial demarcation or stock control.

A   *Gleann Mór and Gob na h-Airde;*
    general view from W
B   *Structure K, Gleann Mór, from SW*
C   *'St Kilda Farm Steading'*
    (from Ross, A, Scottish Home Industries (1895,
    reprinted 1974), 10)

C

vii   GLEANN MÓR: STRUCTURES. Although more complex and more obviously embodying wheelhouse building traditions, the nucleated buildings in Gleann Mór appear to be of the same species as the surviving cellular structures in the village.

The 'Amazon's House' or Taigh na Banaghaisgeich (No. **26**),[61] for example, which is set partly within the slope of the hill, has a central chamber and linked cells, all roofed with turf-covered corbelling. Partly dismantled at one stage and now seriously decaying, this building was already a subject of legend by 1697. Martin Martin also related that 'some of the inhabitants dwell in it all summer, though it be some

hundred years old'.[62]* Whether or not that was an exact and well-informed estimate, the dates of this building and its neighbours remain to be firmly established. They have been claimed as prehistoric, but all that can be confidently asserted on the basis of survey and historical evidence is that the 'Amazon's House' is of about 1600 AD or earlier.

Other buildings of the 'Amazon's House' type appear to have been modified for later use, receiving dykes or 'horns' enclosing an outer forecourt (Nos. **27–30**). Some of these so-called 'horned structures', which have been classified and tentatively attributed to the Iron Age,[63] are of a single period of construction (No. **25**), but most of them overlie older cellular foundations. They are probably better under-

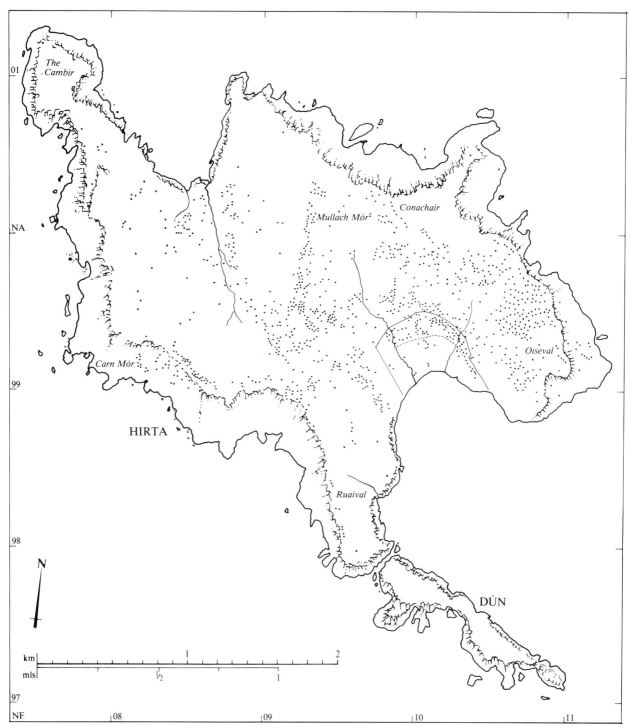

Hirta; distribution map of cleitean

stood as gathering folds (Buaile Crothaidh) as Captain Thomas learnt; he was told that 'the huts . . . were for the lambs and kids . . . from whence they were in sight and smell of their dams, but were prevented from sucking'.[64] Perched on top of these structures, and partly built out of them, are groups of relatively modern cleitean.

viii CLEITEAN AND BOTHIES. A cleit is a small drystone building which is generally straight-sided and of an elongated rectangular form.[65]* The rubble walls are slightly corbelled and the building is roofed by slabs, usually with an earth and turf capping. The inner face tends to be of fairly open construction; the outer wall is more densely built and battered. Martin and other commentators referred to them as 'stone pyramidal houses' or 'pyramids',

and described their general structural characteristics: drystone-built in an open manner, partly corbelled, slab-ceiled with a turf cover, and usually timberless.

Most cleitean are built on a slope, the long axis being aligned with the slope and the entrance usually being placed at the uphill end (e.g. No. **15**). For the most part they occupy dry locations which take advantage of the wind, including updraughts on steep slopes. Indeed, they have been built on slopes of up to thirty degrees, but most structures have a step down just inside the doorway so that the floor, although sloping, is more level than the ground outside. Only one (Cleit 8), however, has a flight of steps down into the interior.

Cleitean are the most numerous structures on the islands. In 1697 Martin Martin estimated that there were

28

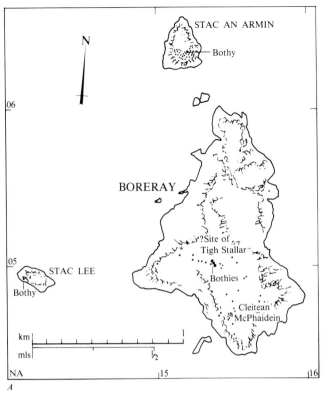

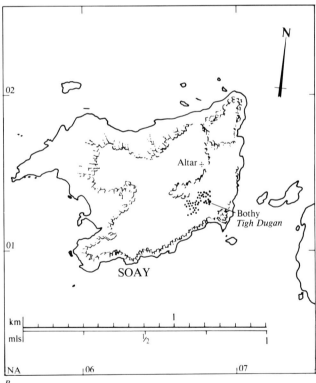

Distribution maps of cleitean and bothies
A   Boreray and Stacs
B   Soay

'some hundreds' on Hirta, 'about 40' on Boreray, 'several' on Stac an Armin, and one on Stac Lee which also served as a bothy.[66] A survey by Mary Harman has produced records of about 1,260 cleitean on Hirta, and over 170 on the other islands and Stacs. Not all these structures were in use at any one time, however, for some are merely foundations adjacent to a cleit which was probably built when its predecessor decayed or collapsed. The modern census also includes bothies and 'lean-to' shelters that were constructed simply by adding walls beneath overhanging rocks; they occur mainly on Carn Mór and Dùn.

There are many cleitean in and around the village, and on the surrounding slopes of Oiseval, Conachair, and the E flank of Mullach Sgar. There are also groups along the ridges running from Mullach Sgar and a significant scatter on the steep slopes to the S of the ridge between Mullach Sgar and Mullach Bi, and on the E side of Oiseval. In Gleann Mór they are distributed mostly on the valley floor, but there are scarcely any on Ruaival or on the slopes N of Mullach Mór and Conachair. There are none on Dùn, but Soay has about forty, Boreray fifty, and Stac an Armin eighty.

Surviving cleitean are of several shapes and sizes, ranging from small roundish structures to elongated round-cornered rectangles which resemble petrified peat-stacks. The largest are in the village, where some entrances in the end-walls are associated with overdoor openings (e.g. No. **15**). There are also a number with side-entrances (e.g. No. **16**), but the positions of a few of these openings are the result of later alterations. A number of village cleitean also preserve fragments of wooden doors and door-frames dating from late phases of use. Some doors have had either pintle or leather hinges, and one complete specimen of harr-hung type, which has survived for over fifty years, is of ledged and battened construction, the battens being roughly adzed and the ledges nailed.

Outside the area of the village, cleitean display less variety in size and most have end-doors. In order to exclude livestock, the entrances to most of these outlying cleitean were probably secured and blocked by one or more large stone slabs, a few of which remain *in situ*. Some cleitean are known to have been owned by individuals, who were responsible for making them stock-proof, and if another person's beast became trapped in a cleit, the cleit-owner had to pay compensation for its injury or death.[67]

Cleitean were used as stores for harvested crops, corn, hay, and latterly potatoes; they also contained dried birds and fish, and eggs preserved in peat ash. Some in the village were used for storing manure. Many cleitean on the hills and ridges were used for storing turf, and some structures still contain cut turves.

Macaulay referred to the fact that 'the inhabitants secure their peats, eggs and wildfowl within these small repositories: every St Kildan has his share of them in proportion to the extent of land he possesses or the rent he pays to the steward . . .'.[68] Mackenzie reckoned that 'some families will have as many as twenty of these [cleitean] full of peat, and also perhaps a score of little stacks outside . . . carried home by the women in creels as required'.[69] That estimate would account for about 400 structures on Hirta for that particular purpose in the 1830s.

Among the fifty surviving cleitean on Boreray the greatest cluster is that on the SW-facing slopes, which was 'seen at some distance' by Martin Martin.[70] In fact, only for Boreray is there record of people staying for any length of time: parties of men went there to work with the sheep and to collect birds and eggs, while groups of girls stayed to 'make feathers' from the intensive catching and plucking of puffins. The three surviving bothies on Boreray are of a semi-subterranean character.

The bothies and shelters on Stac an Armin and Soay are generally free-standing structures. According to Martin,

A

B

A   *Cleitean at E end of village from NW*
B   *in 1938*

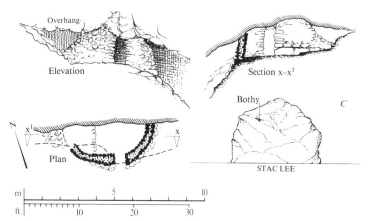

C   *Bothy, Stac Lee*

A *St Kilda 'Parliament', 1886*

'the several stone pyramids' on Stac an Armin were 'as well
for lodging the inhabitants that attend the seasons of the
solan geese [gannets], as for those that preserve and dry
them. . . They brought off 800 of the preceding year's solan
geese dried in their pyramids'.[71] Eighty such structures have
been noted in recent times on the S and SE slopes of the
Stac; if they had been in existence in 1697, these cleitean
would have had an average capacity of about ten gannets,
as well as serving as bothies.

Martin was shown a bothy mid-way up Stac Lee, 'the
stone pyramid house which the inhabitants built for
lodging themselves in . . . in August'. At that season of
the seafowling harvest, just before the gannets and their
grown young flew away for the winter, the sea could be
unpredictably rough, thus delaying the St Kildans' return
voyage to the village. This bothy, about 3 m long inside, is
built under an overhang on a platform which ascends
diagonally across the S face of the Stac.[72] It has a doorway-
opening, with no obvious means of blocking, and there is a
vent in the roof, but no traces of smoke-blackening. The
bothy is not known to have been reconstructed since the
17th century.

POPULATION EVIDENCE

It is natural to assume that whilst the outward forms of the
buildings may have changed, the people of these islands
remained fairly constant in their nature, outlook and ways
of life, especially given the isolated, harsh and special
circumstances of St Kilda. But just how native were the last
generations of native St Kildans, and how continuous were
the human traditions of these islands?[73]

According to Martin, the men of St Kilda 'have
generally but very thin beards, and those too do not appear
till they arrive at the age of thirty, and in some not till after
thirty five; they have all but a few hairs upon the upper lip
and point of the chin'.[74] Such an appearance forms a
complete contrast with the luxuriant beards and whiskers
seen, for instance, in views of a St Kildan 'Parliament', so

how could a basic characteristic of an isolated people have
changed so completely in two centuries?

Much of the answer to this genetic question lies in a
smallpox epidemic of about 1729 which evidently reduced a
population of about 200 to thirty, comprising only four
male adults.[75] Eleven of these, three adults and eight boys,
had been accidentally marooned on Boreray at that time,
and upon their eventual return found only one adult and
eighteen children surviving on Hirta.

There are indications of active resettlement in the 1730s,
bringing the population back up to eighty-eight by the time
of Macaulay's visit in 1758.[76] There is no evidence of
further substantial immigration, but it was presumably
these post-smallpox settlers, mainly from Harris, Uist and
Skye, who were responsible for breeding out the beardless
characteristics of the population. It is also probable that
this resettlement dislocated older traditions, and has given
the buildings in Gleann Mór a greater mystery in folk
memory than they might otherwise have had.

So far as dwellings in the village are concerned, it is

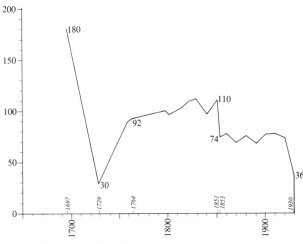

B *St Kilda population 1697–1930*

31

Finlay MacQueen snaring puffins, 1938

reasonable to conclude that 'When St Kilda was resettled after the smallpox of 1729 it seems rather improbable that the resettlers would have used the existing houses, bearing in mind the fear of "fever houses" even now displayed in Hebridean villages. More likely they would build new houses, but these would probably still be in the area of the earlier village.'[77] Although smallpox is unlikely to have been called 'fever', a demographic disaster of this proportion would have provoked a response on the part of the island community similar to that which cholera and typhus produced on the mainland and in other Hebridean villages.

The dire events of the late 1720s may thus be crucial to an understanding of the people and buildings of St Kilda. But this and other aspects of its history can still only be guessed at, despite the fact that it is probably the most written-about island group in Britain. However, that very mystery, allied to the islands' physical grandeur and outstanding natural history, will always be among St Kilda's great powers of attraction.

NOTES

1   *Inventory of the Outer Hebrides*, p. vi.
2   Ibid., No. 158.
3   Monro, *Western Isles*, 77–8.
4   Martin, *Voyage*.
5   Mackenzie, *Life*, 21. See also Acland, A, *A Devon Family, the Story of the Aclands* (1981), 50, 63.
6   Martin, *Voyage*, 10, 11, 16.
7   NLS, Advocates MS 33.3.20, f.21v, 28v.
8   Macaulay, *History*, 42.
9   Brougham, H (Lord), *Memoirs of the Life and Times of Lord Brougham* (1871), **1**, 104. Campbell's map shows the village as a dense cluster of houses between Conachair and the bay. It was published in 1807 in Aaron Arrowsmith's Map of Scotland.
10 Mackenzie, *Life*, 20–1.
11 MacCulloch, *Western Islands*, **2**, 28.
12 Mackenzie, *Life*, 19.
13 Martin, *Voyage*, 10–11.
14 Macaulay, *History*, 43, 44.
15 Otter, W (ed.), *The Life and Remains of Edward Daniel Clarke* (1824), 270 (referring to a visit in 1797).
16 Mackenzie, *Life*, 20.
17 Ibid., 21.
18 Macaulay, *History*, 30.
19 Ibid., 31.
20 Mackenzie, *Life*, 21.
21 Royal Museum of Scotland, Society of Antiquaries of Scotland MS 158, scale 1 in: 100 ft. For other work undertaken by Sharbau in association with Captain Thomas, see Thomas, F W L, in *PSAS*, **3** (1857–60), 127–44, and Ashmore, P, in Breeze, D J (ed.), *Studies in Scottish Antiquity* (1984), 1–31 at 15–17.
22 Thomas, F W L, in *PSAS*, **7** (1870), 153–95 at 155 and pl. 28, fig. 2.
23 Lawson MS, Chapter 2, pp. 13–14.
24 Morgan, J E, in *British and Foreign Medico-Chirurgical Review*, **29** (1862), 191.
25 Buchanan, *Album*.
26 Atkinson, R, *Island Going* (1949), 226–78 and pls 26–35.
27 Mathieson, J, and Cockburn, A M, Map of St Kilda or Hirta, scale 6 in: 1 mile (1928).
28 Williamson, *Summer*, 32–45; Spackman, R A, *Soldiers on St Kilda* (1982), 13–30.
29 For example, MacGregor, D R, in *Scottish Studies*, **4** (1960), 1–48; University of Keele, Department of Extra-Mural Studies, 1966 (Typescript reports lodged with the National Trust for Scotland and the Nature Conservancy Council); Ordnance Survey, Archaeology Division, 1967; Cottam, M B, 1973–4, summarised in Small, *Handbook*, 36–61.
30 Fenton, A, *The Northern Isles: Orkney and Shetland* (1978), 100–5.
31 Mackenzie, *Life*, 7.
32 MacCulloch, *Western Islands*, **2**, 24. St Kilda remained part of the Dunvegan estate until 1779 when, along with Harris, it was sold to Captain Alexander MacLeod, a merchant seaman. He in turn sold St Kilda to another branch of the MacLeod family before it was re-purchased by MacLeod of MacLeod in 1835.
33 NLS, National Map Library MS 5862 9. Appendix IV of the 1826 Annual Report of the Society for the Support of Gaelic Schools reported that Robert Stevenson had furnished the committee with a plan and specification for the erection of a chapel and dwelling house for a Missionary on St Kilda, 'and steps are taken for getting estimates for completing the work' with the help of the proprietor and the Reverend John MacDonald.
34 In the possession of Sir Richard Dyke Acland, College, Broadclyst, Exeter, Devon.
35 MacCulloch, *Highlands*, **3**, 177.
36 Martin, *Voyage*, 43. See also NLS, Adv. MS 33.3. 20, ff. 21v (where six chapels are listed), 28v.
37 Macaulay, *History*, 70–1.
38 Harman, M, in *PSAS*, **108** (1976–7), 254–8.
39 Mackenzie, *Life*, 23.
40 Williamson, *Summer*, 63–4.
41 Ibid., 64.

42 Whitaker, I R, in *Gwerin*, **1** (1956–7), 161–70.
43 Martin, *Voyage*, 53.
44 Wilson, J, *A Voyage round the Coasts of Scotland and the Isles* (1842), **2**, 38.
45 Smith, R A, *A Visit to St Kilda in the 'Nyanza'* (1879), 144.
46 Emery, N, *Excavations in the Village Street, Hirta, St Kilda* (Typescript report, University of Durham, Department of Archaeology, 1986).
47 Buchanan, *Album*, 49.
48 *PSAS*, **7** (1870), pl. 28, fig. 2.
49 Fenton, A, and Hendry, C, in *Review of Scottish Culture*, **1** (1984), 11–28; Hay, G D, in *Post-Medieval Archaeology*, **12** (1978), 125–7.
50 Muir, T S, *St Kilda, a Fragment of Travel* (1858), 13.
51 Mackenzie, *Life*, 18–19.
52 Laing, D, in *PSAS*, **10** (1872–4), 722–30; ibid., **11** (1874–6), 593–608; ibid., **12** (1876–8), 312–13; Sands, J, *Out of the World, or Life in St Kilda* (1878), 106; Marshall, R K, *Virgins and Viragos* (1983), 201–4.
53 Crawford, I A, in *Scottish Archaeological Forum*, **6** (1974), 1–16; idem, and Switsur, R, in *Antiquity*, **51** (1977), 124–36; Ritchie, A, in *PSAS*, **108** (1976–7), 174–227. Cf. also some of the structures on North Rona (Nisbet, H C, and Gailey, R A, in *The Archaeological Journal*, **117** (1962), 88–115).
54 Sands, J, in *PSAS*, **12** (1877), 186–92 at 186–7; Kearton, R, *With Nature and a Camera* (1897), 13; Mathieson, J, in *PSAS*, **62** (1927–8), 123–32 at 125–6; *Inventory of the Outer Hebrides*, No. 158; Williamson, *Summer*, 57–8. The writers are indebted to Mr P R Ritchie, who undertook the most recent excavations, for information about the finds. See also Descriptive List No. 23 below.
55 NMRS Record Card NF 19 NW 18 (Ordnance Survey, Archaeology Division, Davidson, J L, 1967); Cottam, M B, in Small, *Handbook*, 36–61 at 39–45. On the W flank of the arena there is also a mounded structure of indeterminate character that had previously not been detected.
56 Cottam, loc. cit.
57 Macaulay, *History*, 39.
58 Ibid., 29–30, 39.
59 Mackenzie, *Life*, 7.
60 Heathcote, J N, *St Kilda* (1900), 76; reproduced also in Buchanan, *Album*, 57.
61 Muir, T S, and Thomas, F W L, in *PSAS*, **3** (1857–60), 225–32; Mathieson, J, in *PSAS*, **62** (1927–8), 123–32 at 128–30.
62 Martin, *Voyage*, 15. The description continues 'the whole is built of stone, without any wood, lime, earth, or mortar to cement it, and is in the form of a circle pyramid-wise towards the top with a vent in it, the fire being always in the centre of the floor; the stones are long and thin, which supplies the defect of wood: body of this house contains not above nine persons sitting; there are three beds or low vaults at the side of the wall, which contains five men each, and are separated by a pillar . . .'.
63 Williamson, K, in *Scottish Field*, **105** (March 1958), 46–9; idem, *Summer*, 67–75; Cottam, op. cit., 53–61.
64 *PSAS*, **7** (1870), 176.
65 There are few known parallels to the cleitean of St Kilda elsewhere in Scotland; cf., for example, the hut below Beinn a'Chaisteal, Islay, *Inventory of Argyll*, **5**, No. 131.
66 Martin, *Voyage*, 22, 24, 25.
67 Buchan, A, *A Description of St Kilda* (1732 edition reprinted 1974), 27.
68 Macaulay, *History*, 48.
69 Mackenzie, *Life*, 10–11.
70 Martin, *Voyage*, 24.
71 Ibid., 25.
72 Ibid., 22. The authors are grateful to Peter Moore and Stuart Murray for details of this structure; see also Moore, P, in Scottish Vernacular Buildings Working Group, *Vernacular Building*, **11** (forthcoming).
73 This section is based upon the unpublished researches of William Lawson, Stornoway, to whom the authors are much indebted. See also Clegg, E J, in *Northern Scotland*, **6** (1984–5), 3–10.
74 Martin, *Voyage*, 37.
75 Macaulay, *History*, 196–8.
76 Ibid.
77 Lawson MS, Chapter 3, The Village, p. 1.

1A Storehouse from NW
(in course of restoration)

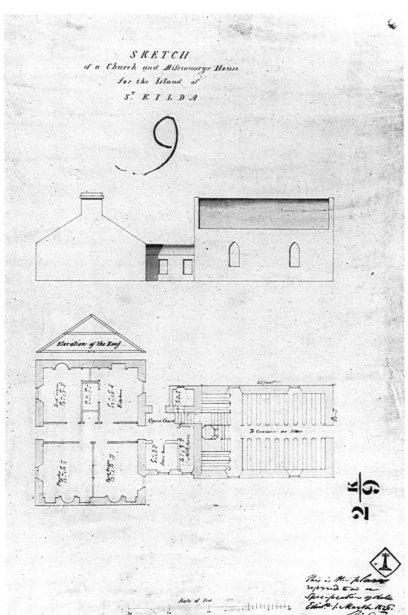

2A Church and Manse;
design drawings, 1826

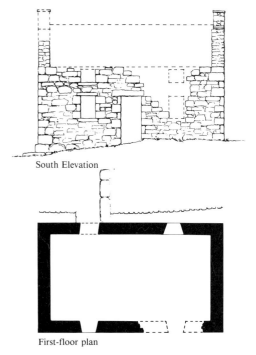

South Elevation

First-floor plan

Ground-floor plan

m |———————————5———————————10
ft. |————10————20————30

1B   Storehouse

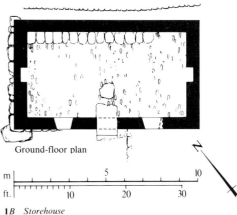

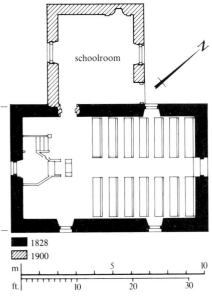

schoolroom

■ 1828
▨ 1900

m |———————————5———————————10
ft. |————10————20————30

2B   Church and School

DESCRIPTIVE LIST

See Editorial Notes for systems of annotation and for correlation with earlier codes of numbers and letters.

1   Storehouse, Village
    NF 1040 9904   NF 19 NW 21.1
This two-storeyed and gabled building stands close to the SE shore of Village Bay, facing SW. The roof and the E half of its three-bay frontage were damaged by gunfire from a German U-boat in May 1918, but a recent programme of restoration has led to the restitution of the damaged front wall and the re-roofing of the structure for use as bothy accommodation.

Marked as 'storehouse' on Sharbau's plan of 1858–60, the building was originally erected some time before 1819, when a visitor noted that 'church service is performed in a house that was erected as a store for the wool and feathers of the natives'.

The building is rectangular on plan, measuring 10·1 m in length by 5·7 m transversely over walls 0·6 m in average thickness. The masonry is lime-mortared rubble which is partly laid to courses and is neatly dressed at the quoins and margins to all openings. Founded partly on a project-ing footings-course and partly on bare rock at the front and sides, the walls are set into the slope of the hillside at the rear, where there is a revetted drainage-ditch.

There is a ground-level entrance in the centre of the SW side-wall, and surviving original window-openings in the W bay have through splays which show the positions of erstwhile frames. The first floor also has a window in the rear wall, and towards the W end of that wall there is a doorway which has a stepped and bridged approach across the drainage-ditch. All the openings are lintelled. Chimney-stacks at the apex of each gable have squared drip-courses and stepped verges above plain gable copes.

Inside, the ground floor is cobbled, and there is a slab-covered drain running along the inner face of the rear wall. Fireplaces with straight ingoings are placed at each end of the ground floor. The upper floor, which has been timber-joisted, appears to have been reached independently by the rear doorway, and there is no clear evidence of the nature or position of an internal stair.
—   See Introduction n. 32.

2   Church, School and Manse, Village
    NF 1035 9910   NF 19 NW 21.2
Its restoration completed in 1980, the church is an oblong and gabled structure which occupies a position on the E edge of the army camp. It is aligned NE–SW and the entrance is in the landward-facing NE gable-wall. The rubble masonry walls are rendered with cement and lime and the roof is slated, there being no exposed gable copes or freestone dressings. The building is of two window bays, and the windows and doorway have arch-pointed heads.

Measuring 10·7 m in length by 6·8 m transversely over walls 0·7 m thick, it conforms almost exactly to the dimens-ions of 35 ft (10·67 m) and 22 ft 4 in (6·81 m) specified on Robert Stevenson's design-drawing of 1826. That drawing shows that the church was intended to contain 106 sitters in nine pairs of pews flanking a central aisle, with two further pairs on each side of an octagonal pulpit at the SW end. The present arrangement consists of seven pairs of bench-pews facing a relatively large pulpit which was introduced into the church after the First World War.

A schoolroom wing was added on the NW side between 1897 and 1900. It is a gabled structure with a doorway in

2C

2D

2E

Church, School and Manse;
  2C *view from N, 1938*
  2D *view from E*
  2E *view from SE, 1938*

the re-entrant angle, and one of the church windows was altered to form a communicating doorway. The interior of the schoolroom measures 4·7 m by 4·1 m, and there is a fireplace set towards the N corner of the NW gable-wall.

The former manse, which now serves as the Sergeants' Mess, has not been surveyed in detail. The external appearance of the building suggests that it contains a linear arrangement of at least three main rooms. The drawing of 1826, on the other hand, shows that it was intended to be of a four-square plan, consisting of two bedrooms, a parlour and a kitchen, all opening off a central transverse corridor. It was linked by a passage to a minister's door at the SW end of the church.

From 1864 until 1930 the bell of the wrecked Greenock-registered SS *Janet Cowan* served as the church bell, and a modern Greenock-made bell now stands in a wooden belfry-frame close to the entrance to the church.

— See Introduction nn. 33–7.

2F

2G

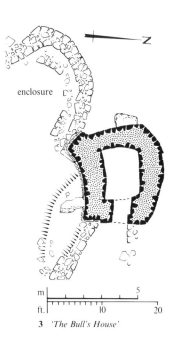

enclosure

Interiors, 1938
2F Church
2G Schoolroom

m _____ 5
ft. _____ 10 _____ 20

3 'The Bull's House'

3 'The Bull's House', Village
NF 1001 9956   NF 19 NW 21.3

This small drystone building lies in an area NW of Tobar Childa, and, comparable in some respects with the houses built in the 1830s, it is the only oblong gabled structure outside the head dyke. Mr Lachlan MacDonald has confirmed that in the 19th century it was built on common land for the bull that was sent to St Kilda by the Department of Agriculture. Similar buildings for housing a township bull exist on common grazings elsewhere in the Hebrides at, for example, Grenitote, North Uist, and Breakish, Skye.

The building measures internally 2·85 m in length from E to W by 1·93 m transversely. The walls are up to 1·3 m thick, and the gable-walls rise to a height of 1·98 m. Because of a fall in ground-level the S side-wall stands to an external height of 2·24 m, and the SW angle is buttressed in relation to the enclosure-wall; the other end of the S wall abuts the E gable and there is no bonding in the lower courses on the inner face. The lintelled doorway in the centre of the E gable-wall is 1·25 m high and 0·89 m wide. In the interstices of the inner face of the N side-wall there are small pieces of dried cattle dung.

In a photograph of 1886 this structure appears thatched and without gables, and the ruinous enclosure with which it is now associated was then complete, having since been dismantled, probably to build Cleit 141 nearby.

4 House 8 and Black House I, Village
NF 1010 9937   NF 19 NW 21.4

The ruinous shell of House 8, which was inhabited by the MacDonald family, exhibits evidence of the features and the standard layout on which, with minor variations, all houses of the 1860s were built. They generally contained a kitchen and room, flanking a central entrance-lobby and closet. Gabled and built of lime-mortared stone, some of which has been dressed, the house is rectangular on plan, measuring 8·92 m by 3·96 m internally. It has a symmetrical three-bay S or street frontage, comprising a central doorway and a pair of window-openings. Parts of a footings-course are visible along the front and E gable-wall, and at the rear of the house there is a revetted drainage channel which forms the S edge of a walled garden.

Internally, the entrance-lobby has had a concrete floor, and the NE corner of the building is also concrete-floored. There are surviving patches of wall plaster and at the W end of the N side-wall the plaster bears traces of a pink wash. There is a fireplace in each gable-wall; the E fireplace has an iron bar built into the ingoing and incorporates a large slab hearthstone. There is a mural cupboard in the SE corner.

Adjacent to the W gable-wall is Black House I, a drystone structure built end-on to the street. Internally, it measures 4·11 m by 1·85 m transversely within walls varying between 0·38 m and 1·22 m in thickness. There is a very large boulder in the NE corner. The walls, which have vertical inner and outer faces and rounded external N angles, rise to a height of 1·65 m at the sides and up to 2·49 m at the gables; because the building is set in to the slope, the N gable-wall is only 1·3 m above ground-level externally. The E side-wall was sagging in 1983, and has since been rebuilt. The entrance is towards the N end of the W side-wall, and is spanned by two slab lintels, the inner lintel still bearing a sheet of roofing zinc. Towards the W end of the S gable-wall is a small window.

At the E end of House 8 archaeological excavations carried out by the University of Durham in 1986, revealed the fragmentary remains of a black house of the 1830s partly underlying the present one. The black house was originally about 10 m in length overall from N to S by

37

4A

4C

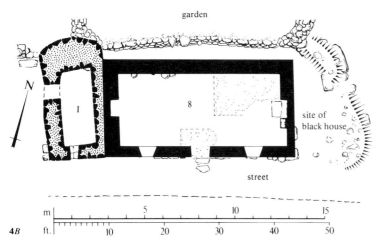

4B

about 6·5 m transversely. Traces of a stone-lined open hearth in the clay floor of the N half of the building were uncovered, and the footings of a cross-wall divided off the area of the former dwelling from the byre at the slightly lower S end.

— See Introduction n. 46; Lawson MS.

5   Black House C, Village
NF 1021 9934   NF 19 NW 21.5

This ruinous drystone building, a typical black house, lies obliquely between Houses 3 and 4, part of its S end-wall forming an edge to the street. Contiguous with the upper N end and set at a slightly higher level, corresponding to the natural slope of the ground, there is a small, transversely aligned annexe. Black House C, together with House 3, was a residence of the Gillies family until the end of the 19th century.

The main structure measures 6·4 m by 3·35 m within walls varying between 1·37 m and 1·9 m in thickness and up

to 1·98 m in height. Externally, the walls are battered and the angles rounded, the S end-wall being almost in the form of an arc on plan. Internally, the N end-wall is not bonded into the side-walls. The doorway is situated towards the S end of the E side-wall, its neatly paved threshold covering what is probably a drain. A little to the N of it is a small window-opening, the sill of which has been levelled with mortared slates in order to fit a window-frame about 0.2 m from the inner wall-face. At the N end of the building traces of red ash from burnt turf or peat are visible in the masonry joints on the lower courses of the wall. At the S end there are two iron rings low down in the W side-wall, and a drain runs out under the end-wall.

The N annexe is set into the slope and the N side-wall is only 0·23 m above ground level. Internally, it measures 3·76 m by 2·26 m within walls varying between 0·99 m and 1·37 m in thickness. The E gable-wall survives to an original height of 2·59 m, and contains a doorway and a window. The doorway, which was formerly fitted with a wooden door-frame, is spanned by two large stone lintels and has a

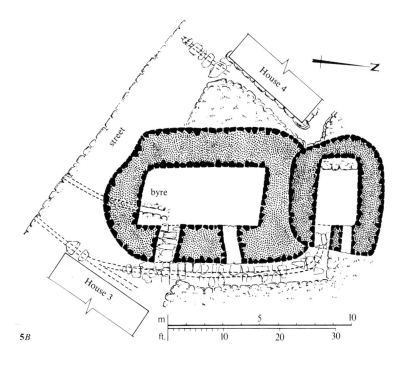

5C

5D

Black House C:
5B   plan
5C   window embrasure
5D   quern-stone in window embrasure

flagged threshold covering a drain. A gneiss quernstone has been built into the N ingoing of the window-opening, and surviving traces of cement and fragments of window-glass suggest that a glazed frame was latterly set about 0·23 m from the inner wall-face. At the W end of the building there is a low platform with a slabbed surface 0·6 m wide and 0·25 m above floor-level.

A flagstone path leads down to the street from the doorways of the two buildings, and a drain from the upper building runs beneath the path to emerge on the S side of the street.

— Lawson MS.

6   Black House E, Village
NF 1016 9936   NF 19 NW 21.6

This ruinous range, possibly the last black house to have been erected on St Kilda, consists of two houses aligned in

series on a slope with the lower S end fronting the street. On the E side a slabstone path runs from the door of the upper building down to the street. On the evidence of Sharbau's plan, this black house did not exist in 1860, and was probably built shortly afterwards for the newly-married Donald Ferguson, eldest son of the family in House 4. Together with its replacement, House 5, it would have subsequently passed to his son, Neil Ferguson.

The S unit measures 5·49 m by 3·05 m transversely within walls varying between about 1 m and 1·9 m in thickness. The side-walls stand to a maximum height of just over 2 m, and the S gable-wall is 2·9 m high. Externally, the angles of the building are rounded and the walls are battered. The doorway is towards the S end of the E side-wall, and a little to the N is a window. Fragments of zinc sheeting are visible above the lintels of both openings, and there are patches of tar and tarred cement on the wall-heads. An iron ring and a bent iron bar in the W side-wall

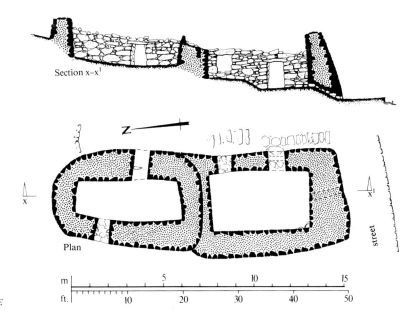

6A   Black House E

close to the SW corner were probably for tethering beasts, and there is a drain which runs under the S wall and on to the street.

The adjacent N unit stands at a slightly higher level, following and partly set into the natural slope of the ground, the N end-wall being no more than 0·99 m in external height. Internally, this building measures 5·82 m in length by 2·24 m within walls varying between 0·99 m and 1·35 m in thickness; the N gable-wall survives to a height of 2·13 m. A lintelled doorway with a neatly paved threshold occupies a position towards the S end of the E side-wall, and there is a window at the N end of the W side-wall; it retains traces of a cement setting for a window-frame.
— Lawson MS.

7 Black House G, Village
NF 1011 9936   NF 19 NW 21.7

This drystone structure lies end-on to the street, and, as with Black House C, there is a smaller, transversely aligned building contiguous with its upper N end. Black House G and its successor, House 7, were occupied by the Gillies family.

The main unit measures 6·76 m by 2·9 m within walls up to 1·6 m thick; the side-walls stand to a height of 1·83 m, while the gables are 2·9 m high, the external angles of the S end-wall being rounded and the narrower upper parts of the gables being later additions. Cement and tar along the wall-heads indicate the edges of the last roof. The doorway is near the S end of the E side-wall and beneath its paved threshold runs a drain. The lintels of the window-opening a little to the N in the same wall are missing. Two pieces of iron project from the W side-wall near the floor; neither has a ring but they are likely to have been used for tethering beasts. A drain runs beneath the S end-wall and under the street. At the N end the lower parts of the adjacent inner wall-faces are not bonded, and there is a large lintel-like stone in the N end-wall but no clearly defined associated jambs.

Internally, the N unit measures 3·74 m by 2·62 m, the walls being up to 1·22 m thick and the angles rounded. The doorway, which is at the S end of the E wall, has outer and inner lintels of stone and timber respectively, and contains the post and lintel of a wooden door-frame. At the W end of the interior there is a narrow platform 0·28 m high. Part of the S side-wall, adjacent to the N gable of the main

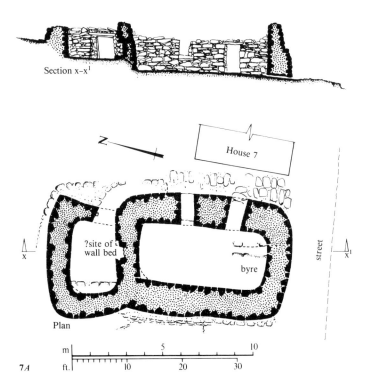

Section x–x¹

House 7

?site of wall bed

byre

street

x   x¹

Plan

m   5   10
ft.   10   20   30

7A

7B

Black House G;
7A plan and section   7B E side-wall

7C *Black House G;*
    wooden door-post
    and lintel

building, collapsed in 1984, revealing part of a lintelled aperture and wall-face within the thickness of the wall.[1] This probably represents the remains of a passage leading into a *crùb* or wall-bed, the newly revealed wall-face probably being part of the inner wall of the bed chamber itself. The chamber was presumably destroyed when the N building was added, and the *crùb* entrance covered or removed when the N wall of the main building was re-faced, hence the lack of bonding at the internal angles. This building is noted on Sharbau's plan as having a bed in the wall.

On the E side of the building a paved path leads from the upper doorway past the lower entrance to the street. On the W side a small stream is canalised between Black Houses G and H and runs through a culvert to emerge on the S side of the street.

[1] This wall was subsequently rebuilt and the vestigial *crùb* entrance immured.
— Lawson MS.

8   Black House K, Village
NF 1008 9935   NF 19 NW 21.8

Standing immediately W of House 9, the roofless remains of this house occupy the NE angle at the junction of the street and the path to the burial-ground. It was probably erected by Calum MacDonald soon after his marriage in 1834 to Betty Scott from Lochinver. It can be identified as 'Betty Scott's Cottage' surveyed in the 1860s by Captain

Thomas. Its successor, House 9, continued to be inhabited by the MacDonald family.

The building measures internally 5·94 m from N to S by 3·2 m transversely within side- and end-walls up to 1·37 m and 1·88 m thick respectively. The external angles are rounded except at the NW angle, where there is evidence of rebuilding; the SE angle also appears to have been

8B   *Black House K; interior, N end-wall*

reconstructed, probably in order to accommodate House 9 on the street-line. The drystone walls, which are battered externally and have vertical inner faces, are only 0·61 m high at the N end where the building is set in to the slope. The building has been hip-roofed, and there is no evidence of later superimposed gables. There is a doorway, which has an angled, lintelled entrance-passage, towards the S end of the E side-wall, and to the N of it is a window-embrasure. Inside, the S angles are rounded, but the inner face of the N end-wall is clearly an insertion, not being bonded at the angles. Just below the window sill there is a projecting iron pin, and the inner face of the N end-wall incorporates part of a brick.

Outside, a slabstone path and steps ascend the narrow intervening space between Black House K and House 9.
— See Introduction n. 48; Lawson MS.

9   Black House L, Village
NF 1005 9938   NF 19 NW 21.9

The remains of this building lie to the E of the path leading from the street to the burial-ground. On Sharbau's plan a building on this site is overlaid in darker hatching by a longer structure marked 'Village Barn'. This sequence appears to be reflected in the surviving remains.

Aligned N–S, the building measures internally 3·99 m by 1·93 m within walls which vary in thickness from about 1·15 m to 3 m at the N end where the squared internal angles are not bonded except in the upper few courses. Externally, the walls are battered and the corners rounded. The doorway, which is in the E side-wall, has an entrance-

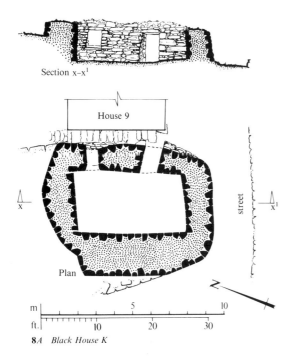

Section x–x[1]

House 9

street

x   x[1]

Plan

m ___ 5 ___ 10
ft. ___ 10 ___ 20 ___ 30

8A   *Black House K*

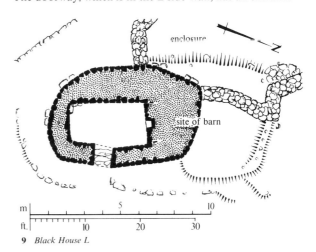

enclosure

site of barn

m ___ 5 ___ 10
ft. ___ 10 ___ 20 ___ 30

9   *Black House L*

passage spanned by three slab lintels, and preserves traces of a wooden door-frame. In the N wall there is an aumbry, roughly 0·33 m in cubic dimensions, but unusually there is no window. At the wall-head there are fragments of wall-plates, and some wire over the doorway may have helped to secure the roof-covering.

A later dyke over-rides the outer edge of the N wall and was probably intended to prevent stock from entering the adjacent enclosure on the NW side. Beyond the N end of the building there are mounded foundations which are apparently earlier than the adjacent enclosure-wall. They probably represent the N extent of the former barn, later foreshortened and re-faced internally.

10 Black Houses M, N and O, Village
   NF 1005 9934   NF 19 NW 21.10
This group of drystone buildings lies end-on to the street, occupying a site between Houses 10 and 11 in the area to the W of the main consumption dyke. Black Houses M and N are contiguous, sharing a common side-wall. It is clear from Sharbau's plan that in 1858 these houses were used by Donald MacQueen and John Gillies. House 10 nearby, which replaced another black house in this group, continued to be occupied by the MacQueens, and House 11 by the Gillies household.

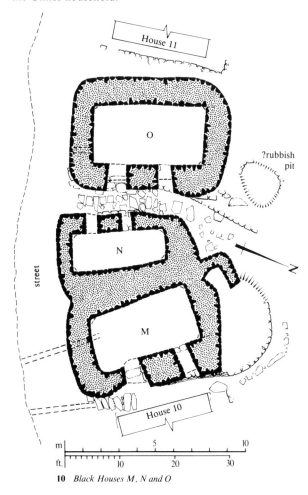

10 *Black Houses M, N and O*

Black House M measures internally 5·64 m by 2·95 m within walls up to 1·7 m thick. Externally, the walls are battered and the corners rounded. At the N end the external wall-face is low because the building is set in to a slope, but the line of an outer face continues at a lower level, curving into a mound. On the NW corner of this mound is a small cleit-like structure, roofed with timber and turf, now mostly collapsed. In the E side-wall of the main building there is a window and doorway, the

doorway-opening retaining the post of a wooden door-frame. Inside, the S angles are rounded and at the squared NE angle the N end-wall is bonded only in its upper courses. A drain, not visible inside, empties on to the street from the centre of the S end-wall. Another drain runs under the flagstones on the E side, and then below the street.

Black House N, virtually a lateral annexe, measures internally 4·98 m in length, its width tapering from 2·03 m to 1·46 m S to N and the walls being up to 1·68 m thick. The external SW angle is square. The doorway, which is near the S end of the W side-wall, has a slabbed threshold and three stone lintels, and there is a window a little to the N in the same wall.

Black House O measures internally 6·13 m by 3·05 m within walls up to 1·42 m thick. Gables have been added to the end-walls which rise to a height of 3·05 m. Rounded externally, the internal angles are square, and the lower halves of the NE, NW and SE angles are not mutually bonded. The N end-wall thus appears to have been partly rebuilt or refaced. Traces of red ash can be found in the interstices of this wall and at the N end of the W side-wall, while in the S gable-wall there is an area of mortared walling. A drain runs beneath this wall on to the street. The doorway, which is near the S end of the E side-wall, has a slabbed threshold and on the inner face there are two large timbers joined to form a lintel. A little to the N in the same wall the inner lintel of the window-embrasure is also of timber with a stone lintel above; the window-frame itself was set about 0·41 m from the inner wall-face. Traces of cement and tar on the wall-heads show the lines of the last roof and roof-timbers.

Outside, a slabstone path runs between Black Houses N and O and continues up the slope past the NE corner, possibly leading to the rubbish pit in that area.
— Lawson MS.

11 Black House W, Village
   NF 1030 9929   NF 19 NW 21.11
Standing in the area E of the Abhainn Ilishgil, mid-way between the street and the head dyke, this building is an unusual rectangular structure aligned with the slope. The upper NW end is reduced to footings, while the lower SE end incorporates a small gabled building which is aligned transversely in relation to the main structure and is shown thatched in photographs of the 1870s and 1886. This building was probably inhabited by either Mary MacCrimmon, a widow, or Effie MacCrimmon, a spinster,

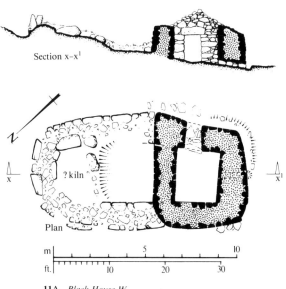

11A *Black House W*

11B Black House W;
doorway in
SE gable-wall

both of whom are recorded as living in this area, the latter until at least 1861.

The interior of the S building measures 2·87 m by about 2·13 m within drystone walls up to 1·78 m thick; the gable-walls stand to an original height of 2·62 m. The doorway is in the E gable-wall; it has a paved sill, and has had a wooden door-frame. In the opposite gable-wall there is a blocked, low-level lintelled opening approximately 0·66 m high by 0·33 m wide. The N side-wall, which retains traces of red ash among the lowest courses of masonry, is not bonded into the gable-walls inside or outside. The floor is unevenly cobbled and there may be a drain along the N side. A drain runs beneath the S wall.

The foundations at the rounded N end include large earthfast stones, and contain a raised platform about 0·76 m above the general level of the interior. On the S edge of this platform there is a slab covering a flue-like channel which penetrates at least 0·78 m into the raised area.

The plan of this building suggests an identification as a corn-drying kiln, the reconstructed portion at the S end perhaps having served as a threshing and winnowing floor. The features are similar to those of other Hebridean kilns, although in this case the suggested kiln-bowl is, unusually, at a higher level than the rest of the building. It is known that the St Kildans had one corn-drying kiln which was held in common.

— See Introduction nn. 40–44; Lawson MS.

12   Cleit 32, Village
NF 1026 9936   NF 19 NW 21.12
This drystone building, which does not conform to the plan of a true cleit, lies to the W of the Abhainn Ilishgil and stands on a steep slope immediately below an old terraced track which runs towards the area of the old village.

The structure is roughly pear-shaped on plan, the apex being at the N end, where the building is set in to the scarp of the old track. At its greatest extent the interior measures 3·81 m by 2·44 m, and because the walls are corbelled the corresponding clear span at the wall-head is 1·93 m. The N and S ends may have had superimposed gables. A lintelled doorway forms an angled passage through the S end of the E side-wall. Towards the N end of the W side-wall there is a blocked low-level and lintelled opening 0·36 m wide and 0·56 m above present floor-level. At this point the external wall-face is inset between two short projecting sections of corbelled walling, which represent the remains of a cell entered from within the main structure. There appears to be a similar blocked aperture at the S end of the W wall but with no obvious traces of an associated cell.

In photographs of 1886 this building is shown thatched, and a view taken in 1957 shows a ridge-pole between the two later gables. At some date after 1886 the door lintel was replaced by a large timber baulk which was in turn replaced by a stone lintel in the mid-1970s. Both these phases of alterations involved much reconstruction of the outer wall-face around the doorway.

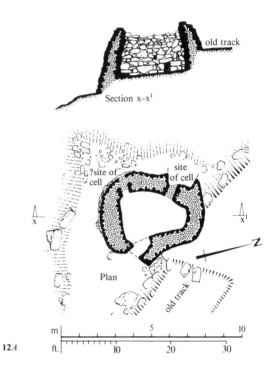

12A

Cleit 32;
12A   plan and section
12B   view from SE, 1957   12B

43

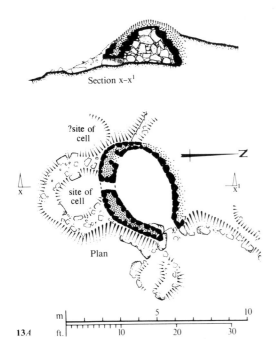

Section x–x¹

?site of cell

site of cell

Plan

13B

Cleit 57
('Calum Mór's House');
  13A   plan and section
  13B   view from E
  13C   interior

13C

13A

m   5   10

ft.   10   20   30

13   Cleit 57 ('Calum Mór's House'), Village
NF 1006 9948   NF 19 NW 21.13

Known since the middle of the 19th century as Calum Mór's House, Cleit 57 stands within the head dyke a short distance NE of the burial-ground. It is oval on plan with evidence of one, possibly two, adjacent cells. Externally, the building appears as a turf-covered mound with an eroded crown 0·91 m above ground-level on the N and 2·75 m on the S. The entrance, which faces E, has two steps (about 0·61 m) down from the exterior, and to the S of it there is a short arc of walling of unknown purpose.

Internally, the building measures 4·57 m from E to W by 2·85 m transversely. The walls are corbelled in a continuous curve, the inner faces of some of the largest stones measuring as much as 1·22 m by 0·41 m. At the crown of the roof a single stone has a clear span of 0·91 m, and nearer the doorway a lower slab spans 1·12 m. Above a floor of rough boulders, some of which are known to have been introduced in 1974, the maximum height is 2·08 m.

On the inner face of the S sector there is a blocked low-level and lintelled aperture 0·31 m high and 0·41 m wide. Externally, the ground drops by about 0·53 m to the 'floor' of a turf-covered subcircular foundation enclosing an area roughly 2·13 m by 1·88 m. Inside, a little further W, there is a blocked aperture 0·56 m high and 0·51 m wide. The lintel is visible externally, but there is no surviving evidence of an associated cell.

The Reverend Neil Mackenzie stated that only one of the earlier houses, occupied by a widow, was left when the village was rebuilt in the 1830s. Since this structure lies within the area probably covered by the older village, it is possible that it is the house in question, although the house-types in use immediately before the Mackenzie rebuilding were thatched, not stone-roofed.

Calum Mór's House is not referred to by that name before the 1860s, even by those writers with an interest in antiquities.

— Mackenzie, *Life*, 20–1; Williamson, *Summer*, 59.

14   Cleit 61, Village
NF 0997 9947   see NF 19 NW 21.14

This drystone structure lies across the head dyke and its door faces down the slope. It is wider than most true cleitean, and though there are no visible traces of attached cells, its general character and position suggest that it is part of a remodelled cellular structure. The fact that the head dyke abuts it clearly indicates that it antedates the 1830s.

Internally, the building measures 3·35 m by 1·91 m within walls up to 1·32 m thick. The corbelled ceiling rises to a height of 1·52 m above the existing floor. A mound outside the doorway drops sharply to the natural slope, and some stones to the N, which form no discernible pattern, may have been associated with this structure.

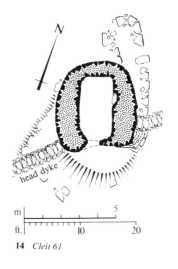

N

head dyke

m   5

ft.   10   20

14   *Cleit 61*

15A

16A

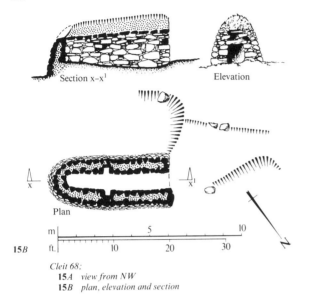

Section x–x¹   Elevation

Plan

m		5		10
ft.	10	20	30	

15B

Cleit 68;
15A   view from NW
15B   plan, elevation and section

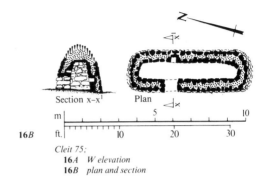

Section x–x¹   Plan

m		5		10
ft.	10	20	30	

16B

Cleit 75;
16A   W elevation
16B   plan and section

15   Cleit 68, Village
NF 1003 9942   NF 19 NW 21.15

This simple drystone structure, a good example of a regular cleit with an end entrance, stands in an area N of the burial-ground close to the W edge of the plot associated with House 10 and Black House M.

Set on a gentle slope, it is aligned NW–SE and of an elongated U-plan, the open entrance end facing uphill. Externally, the walls are battered and built of small stones, the roof consisting of a rounded heap of earth and stones covered with turf. The entrance is of the same internal width as the cleit and there is a further opening 0·31 m high between the door lintel and the ceiling. The E jamb of the doorway preserves traces of a wooden door-frame. Internally, the walls are built mainly of medium-sized stones and are corbelled towards the ceiling where the slabs have an internal clear span of 0·43 m. At and above the level of the existing floor, which incorporates an 0·28 m layer of dung and debris, the width at mid-length is 0·94 m and the height 1·6 m; the cleit interior measures 5·72 m in maximum length.

16   Cleit 75, Village
NF 1002 9940   NF 19 NW 21.16

This drystone structure, a good example of a village cleit with a side entrance, stands in the area NW of the burial-ground. It is built within the plot formerly attached to House 11 and Black House O, its W wall forming part of the boundary of the adjacent strip associated with Black Houses P and Q.

The cleit stands on a gentle slope and is aligned N–S, the entrance being towards the N end of the W side-wall. The building is of an elongated subrectangular plan, straight-sided and round-angled, outside and inside. Externally,

the walls are battered, and the roof, which consists of a covering of turf, earth and stones above a series of slab ceiling-lintels, has a rounded profile. There is what appears to be a small aumbry over the inner face of the doorway. Internally, the walls are built mainly of medium-sized stones except at the S end where the masonry comprises larger blocks and a more open construction. The walls are corbelled and the ceiling-slabs have a clear span of 0·53 m above a floor-level width of 0·99 m. The interior is 5·62 m in maximum length and the height above the existing floor-level is 1·27 m. A more solid, probably stony, floor lies about 0·33 m below the existing level.

17   Cleit 85, Village
NF 1005 9930   NF 19 NW 21.17

The largest surviving cleit S of the street, Cleit 85 is popularly known as Lady Grange's House. Though it may

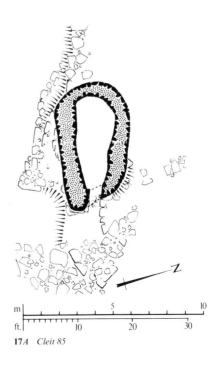

m		5		10
ft.	10	20	30	

17A   Cleit 85

Cleit 85;
   17B *view from SE*   **17C** *interior*

occupy the site of the house in which she resided, it is unlikely to incorporate more than a mere vestige of that structure which in 1876 was reported as having been demolished 'a few years ago'.

The drystone walls are battered externally and are neatly corbelled inside. The building measures internally 4·67 m in length by 2·01 m in maximum width near the W end, where it achieves a height of about 2·44 m; it is narrower and lower towards the doorway at the E end.

The doorway has an inward-sloping inner lintel supported on the S side by a single upright slab and two superincumbent courses. The existing wooden door was constructed and put in position in the late 1970s.

Outside the doorway on the N side there are several paving stones and a step up to the higher ground. To the S the ground falls away steeply below the base of the outer wall and there is some revetting of the slope.

— See Introduction n. 52.

18   Cleitean 122–3, Village

NF 0992 9950   see NF 19 NW 21.18

Cleit 122, which lies well outside the head dyke to the NW of the burial-ground, is the only building in the village area with an intact attached cell (123), the smaller cell being linked by a low-level passage in the NE sector of the parent structure.

The outer walls of Cleit 122 are battered and buttressed on the S side. The doorway is at the W end and has a slight

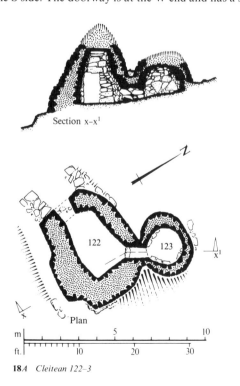

Section x–x¹

Plan

m | 5 | 10
ft. | 10 | 20 | 30

18A *Cleitean 122–3*

Cleitean 122–3;
   18B *view from W*   **18C** *view from E*

outward splay with groups of stones on each side. For a cleit the entrance is tall (1·47 m) and the interior roomy; it is 3·35 m long, 2·21 m wide, and the corbelled walls are lintelled at a height of 2·69 m above the floor. A later wall has been built against the inner face of the E end-wall and the original internal length of the building is likely to have been about 4·25 m.

In the NE corner a low lintelled passage about 0·43 m high, 0·53 m wide, and 1·12 m long gives access to the adjacent subcircular cell. This cell, which measures 2·18 m in maximum diameter, is of corbelled construction, and rises to a height of 1·55 m above the existing floor-level. Above the entrance there is a small opening 0·41 m square, possibly a window and not merely the result of dilapidation.

— Williamson, *Summer*, 59–60.

19   Cleit 137, Village

NF 0999 9954   see NF 19 NW 21.19

Cleit 137, which lies outside the head dyke, is slightly wider internally than most cleitean and at the N end retains the foundations of an attached cell. In a photograph of 1886 this cell is shown complete and roofed.

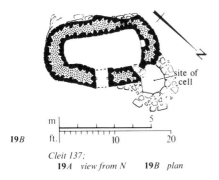

Cleit 137;
19A *view from N* **19B** *plan*

The main body of the cleit is 4·21 m in length and towards the N end achieves a maximum width of 1·88 m. The doorway is in the middle of the NE side-wall. At the NW angle there is a break in the outer wall, which also appears originally to have extended further W at the S end. The untidy aspect of the SW side-wall and the internal narrowing of the S end also betray evidence of reconstruction. Internally, the walls are corbelled and the cleit is ceiled by slab-lintels 1·78 m above floor-level. Within the NW end there is an aumbry and above it an opening, possibly a window, now partly obscured by the external wall-face.

In the N sector a small, low-level opening, 0·28 m high by 0·33 m wide, gives access to the remains of the cell. Up to five corbelled courses of the cell wall survive around this aperture, while the remaining foundations show that the cell has been about 1·83 m in internal diameter.

— Williamson, *Summer*, 62.

20 Cleit 142, Village
NF 1002 9954   NF 19 NW 21.20
This drystone building, which lies outside the head dyke close to Tobar Childa, is of particular interest because it is linked to a ruined cell; compared with a regular cleit it is

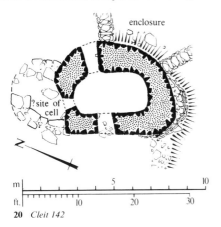

20 *Cleit 142*

also of unusual width and height, and has two entrances, one of which is now blocked. Part of the structure forms the W end of an enclosure which abuts the E side-wall.

Externally, the walls are battered, and they are also revetted on the E and S, where the ground falls away. Internally, the main structure is 3·66 m long and 2·06 m wide. The walls are corbelled and ceiled by large slabs at a height of 2·29 m above floor-level. The doorway now in use is near the middle of the W side-wall and its outer lintels are two stout timbers containing a series of wooden pegs. Towards the N end of the opposite wall there is another blocked doorway which contains an immured timber jamb and lintel. A wall has been added in this area probably in order to discourage stock from entering the adjacent enclosure.

At the N end of the cleit there is a narrow passage 0·36 m high, 0·38 m wide, and 0·81 m long. It leads into a sub-circular cell, which is represented only by foundations and measures 2·29 m in maximum diameter.

— Williamson, *Summer*, 61.

21 Cleitean 144–5, Village
NF 1004 9953   NF 19 NW 21.21
These two drystone buildings, which lie outside the head dyke close to Tobar Childa, stand end to end on a sloping NW–SE axis, both having entrances near the centres of their SW side-walls. While both buildings appear superficially to be ordinary cleitean, they incorporate fragments of an earlier cellular structure.

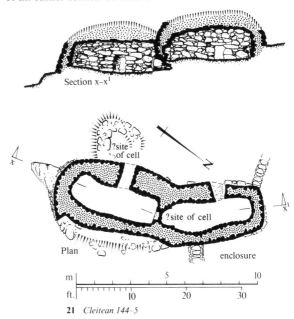

21 *Cleitean 144–5*

Cleit 144, the upper of the two adjacent buildings, forms part of an enclosure at its N end, and, probably to prevent animals scrambling over the cleit into the enclosure, walls were added on the W and SE sides. At its maximum extent the slab-lintelled interior of the building itself is 5·01 m long, 1·52 m wide (in the SE half), and 1·45 m high. At the S end there is a small blocked opening 0·33 m square; its lintel is 0·46 m and 0·91 m respectively above the corresponding floor-levels in 144 and 145, the wall at this point being 0·7 m thick.

Cleit 145 has a battered wall-face and is buttressed at the SE corner. On the S side of the doorway there is a roughly circular setting of stones, possibly the remains of a cell about 1·07 m in diameter. The main structure is 4·57 m long internally, 1·42 m wide, and the lintelled roof is 1·52 m above floor-level. The corbelling is more pronounced on the E side, but at the NE corner the wall is almost vertical to a height of 1·22 m. It abuts the N end-wall, which is noticeably square, whereas the W side-wall is mutually bonded from the lowest courses. In the N end-wall there is an aperture 0·38 m high and 0·18 m above the floor but below the existing floor-level of its neighbour, Cleit 144.

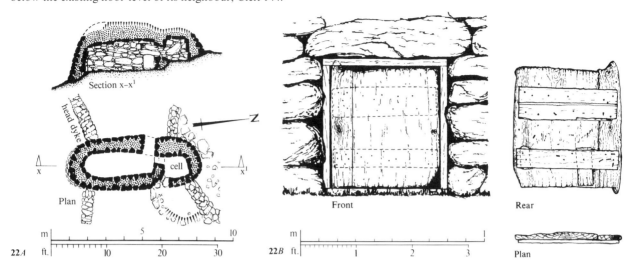

Section x–x¹

head dyke

cell

Plan

m ___ 5 ___ 10
22A ft. ___ 10 ___ 20 ___ 30

Front

Rear

m ___
22B ft. ___ 1 ___ 2 ___ 3

Plan

22 Cleit 155, Village
NF 1006 9950   NF 19 NW 21.22

The head dyke abuts this small drystone structure which also possesses a small cell at the N end. Its position and form thus indicate that it was built before the late 1830s, and it was in this cleit that the only surviving cleit door was found.

Measuring 3·91 m in length by 0·91 m internally, with a lintelled roof 1·45 m above floor-level, the main building is aligned roughly N–S. Unusually, the entrance is in a corner position at the N end of the W side-wall. Externally, the walls are battered and made up of relatively small stones; inside, the masonry consists of fairly large boulders, and the walls are slightly corbelled. The rounded S end traverses the line of the head dyke which abuts the flanking walls.

The W side-wall continues northwards to form a small subcircular cell which measures 1·42 m by 0·99 m transversely, its corbelled roof surviving to a height of 1·04 m. Beside and above the cleit entrance, 0·81 m above the cleit floor, there is a small opening into the cell; the aperture is

0·46 m high and 0·76 m deep. The cell has partly collapsed on the E side where there may be another entrance or an aumbry.

A wall, which forms part of a higher-level enclosure, appears to be bonded into the cleit immediately N of the doorway, and a ruined wall, apparently partly dismantled, adjoins the E side of the cell.

23 Souterrain (Taigh an t-Sithiche) and Cleit 70, Village
NF 1001 9941   NF 19 NW 7 & 21.23

Taigh an t-Sithiche ('House of the Fairies') lies just N of the burial-ground on the strip previously belonging to House 11. Some time after its discovery in about 1844, Sands carried out a detailed investigation. He reported that it was '25 feet [7·62 m] long by about 3 feet 8 inches [1·12 m] wide and about 4 feet [1·22 m] high. The stones with which it is built are large, and the massive walls converge towards the top, so that lintels can be placed on them to form a roof. At a right angle to the house is what I thought to be a passage, but the men declared it to be a *crupa* or bedplace.' In a deposit of peat- or turf-ash on the floor he found

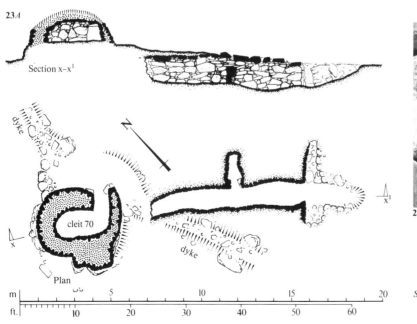

23A

Section x–x¹

dyke

cleit 70

dyke

Plan

m ___ 5 ___ 10 ___ 15 ___ 20
ft. ___ 10 ___ 20 ___ 30 ___ 40 ___ 50 ___ 60

23B

Souterrain and Cleit 70;
  23A *plan and section*
  23B *view from SE, 1949*

23C

23D

Souterrain and Cleit 70;
23C *view from SE*
23D *interior, main passage*

bones of animals and birds, shells, coarse pottery, and stone implements, some used for pounding and some, as he thought, as axes or cleavers. Under the floor there was a drain.

Kearton and Mackenzie also cleared out and 'restored' the structure, finding among other things an iron spearhead. Further excavations were conducted in 1927 by Mathieson and in 1974 by P R Ritchie.

The souterrain survives much as Sands described it: an almost straight subterranean passage aligned NW–SE and 7·6 m in length. At about halfway there is a passage branching 1·83 m to the NE. The entrance of this shorter passage has a width of only 0·66 m and a height of 0·94 m, dimensions usually associated with access to wall-beds. The walls are less regular than those of the main passage. Mathieson considered that there were similar opposed lateral chambers towards the SE end, but the evidence for further chambers is inconclusive. It is from this end that the main passage is now entered (rather than through the roof as in Sands's day), and the masonry around the opening indicates the likelihood of cross-walls in this position. The walls of the main passage continue for a further 2·5 m to the SE, showing that the passage was originally longer in that direction.

It is also likely that the main passage was longer at the N end where it now finishes with a rough face of earth and stones which lies almost directly beneath the strip boundary. It probably ended beneath, or possibly beyond, Cleit 70, which stands on the other side of that boundary, the passage having perhaps been broken into and infilled during the construction of the boundary dyke.

By the standards of village cleitean, Cleit 70 is small and unusual in having its entrance on a corner. Internally, it is 2·87 m long by 1·37 m transversely; it stands to a height of 0·91 m, the floor being at least 0·3 m above the level of the souterrain lintels. On the lower ground to the W several large stones form an arc around the NW corner and the SW corner is buttressed. The external walls of the cleit and

a nearby stone heap on the boundary dyke contain fire-cracked stones, pounders, and a few shaped stones, probably the same as Sands's 'cleavers'.

Some of the finds from the excavations have been deposited in the Royal Museum of Scotland, Queen Street, Edinburgh. A few decorated potsherds are considered to be of standard Iron Age type comparable with pottery found at Clettraval and elsewhere in the Hebrides.
— See Introduction n. 54.

24 Underground Cell, Village
NF 1012 9922   NF 19 NW 21.24

This small stone-lined structure lies in the lower meadows on the boundary between the plots formerly associated with Houses 7 and 8. It is roofed by lintels, two of which are exposed and loose on the ground surface. The subterranean chamber is oval on plan, measuring 1·27 m in maximum length by 0·91 m transversely. The visible remains comprise two courses of masonry, possibly slightly corbelled, standing about 0·4 m above a vegetation-covered floor; the full depth is unknown.

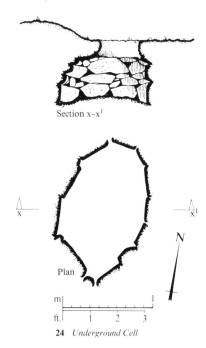

Section x–x[1]

Plan

24 *Underground Cell*

Although its precise nature and purpose cannot be determined without excavation, the structure may possibly be an example of one of the types of ancient burial discussed by Mackenzie, who wrote 'Scattered about, here and there, and very numerous, were green mounds called *gnocan sithichean*, which were looked upon as the abodes of the fairies. These were all removed in the course of agricultural improvements. They were composed of stones mixed with a little earth to a depth of two or three feet. At some distance below this layer were stone coffins formed in two different ways. At times they were formed of four flat stones set on edge and covered by a fifth. At other times both the sides and the roof were formed of several stones set in the same way. These were seemingly of different age from the former. In a few of them bones were found, and in nearly all of them pieces of earthen vessels.'

The structures of the first type are clearly cist-burials and are presumably of Bronze Age or later date. The second type may be compared with the corbelled chamber excavated at Rossinish in Benbecula, which was about 1 m in internal diameter and was partly sunk into the ground, partly covered by a small mound. The contents of this and associated structures indicated a Bronze Age date.
— Mackenzie, *Life*, 6–7; Megaw, J V S, and Simpson, D D A, in *PSAS*, **94** (1960–1), 62–78; Crawford, I A, in *PSAS*, **108** (1976–7), 94–107.

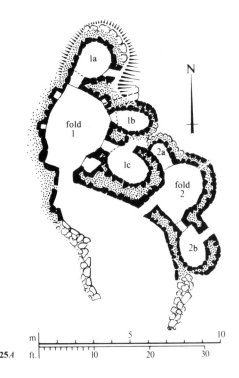

25B

Structure B, Gleann Mór:
25A plan
25B Fold 1 from S, 1957

25A

25   Structure B, Gleann Mór
NF 0855 9983   see NA 00 SE 1
This structure, one of the most southerly of the 'gathering folds' in Gleann Mór, lies in a sheltered hollow on the W side of the glen. It consists of an outer court and two open walled areas or folds, each associated with cells.

The northernmost open area (Fold 1) is of irregular plan, measuring 4·32 m by 3·2 m in maximum length and width; it is enclosed by a drystone wall which stands to a maximum height of 1·22 m and incorporates several upright slabs. The entrance, which faces SW, is 0·76 m wide, and from its threshold slab there is a step down into the fold. On the W side of the entrance a low wall runs to the S, partly forming a revetment against the slope of the hollow. The N and E façades of the outer court are largely made up of the external walls of Cells 1c and 2b, which continue southwards for a short distance in the form of a low rubble dyke.

There are four aumbries in the fold wall, all placed between 0·43 m and 0·76 m above ground-level: two in the NW face are of similar size and position, being about 0·31 m in cubic dimensions; a third aumbry of similar size lies between Cells 1a and 1b; the largest, between Cell 1c and the entrance, widens from 0·36 m to 0·71 m inside and is 0·66 m deep, being roofed by three slabs. Below the third aumbry on the E side of the fold there is a drain which runs eastward.

On the NE side of the fold is Cell 1a which measures 2·08 m by 1·63 m internally and has a corbelled roof at least 1·12 m above floor-level. Its entrance, 0·48 m wide and 0·41 m high, is 0·2 m above ground-level, and on the S side of the cell there is a smaller and partly collapsed opening. Cell 1b, on the SE side, measures 1·7 m by 1·07 m internally, and is entered by an aperture 0·31 m wide, 0·38 m high, and 0·2 m above ground-level. The rear wall has collapsed, but part of the corbelled roof survives to a height of 0·79 m. Immediately adjacent to the W, Cell 1c measures 2·44 m by 1·22 m internally, and is entered through an opening 0·41 m wide, 0·33 m high, and 0·58 m above ground-level. Part of the corbelled roof survives to a height of 1·07 m. On the E side there is a second, external entrance 0·46 m square.

The open area of Fold 2 measures 3·05 m by 2·59 m, with walls up to 0·76 m and 1·07 m in thickness and height. The

entrance is 0·53 m wide, and on the opposite side a drain runs out beneath the E wall. Cell 2a, a very ruined structure, is on the N side of the fold, adjoining Cell 1c. Internally, it measures approximately 1·5 m by 0·89 m, and the entrance is 0·66 m wide. Cell 2b on the S side of the fold has internal dimensions of 2·01 m by 1·45 m, and the corbelled roof stands 0·81 m above floor-level. The cell is entered through an aperture 0·48 m wide, 0·33 m high, and 0·28 m above ground-level. On the E side of the cell there is an external entrance 0·36 m wide.

26   Structure F (including 'Taigh na Banaghaisgeich', the 'Amazon's House'), Gleann Mór
NA 0879 0009   NA 00 SE 2
Occupying a sloping site at the foot of the steeper slopes of Mullach Mór, this is the most complex group of buildings in Gleann Mór. It consists of a 'gathering fold', the 'Amazon's House', another structure of 'Amazon's House' type, and three cleitean (416–18).

The fold at the upper (E) end consists of an open, kidney-shaped area, 4·11 m and 2·29 m in maximum length and width. It is enclosed by a vertically-faced wall and is fronted by a pair of stone dykes which run eastwards and northwards. The entrance-passage, which faces E and splays outward, is 0·61 m wide at the inner end.

26A   Structure F, Gleann Mór, from E

26B *Structure F, Gleann Mòr, from NE, 1957*

Grouped around the fold are three corbelled and sub-circular cells (*a*–*c*). On the N side, Cell *a* measures 1·93 m in diameter and stands to a height of 1·02 m above floor-level; it is entered by a narrow passage 0·47 m high and 0·58 m above ground-level. Cell *b*, which forms the S side of the entrance to the fold, is 1·32 m in diameter and 0·89 m high internally, its entrance being 0·31 m high and 0·71 m above ground-level. Cell *c*, on the W side of the fold, has been reconstructed as a cleit (418). It is 2·52 m in maximum diameter, and in the E flank there is a small entrance 0·36 m

high and 0·81 m above ground-level. The entrance to the cleit as rebuilt is at the S end.

On the slightly higher ground to the SE of the fold there is a relatively large and well-preserved corbelled cell, together with remains of associated cellular structures. The main cell is roughly circular on plan, about 2·2 m in diameter, and stands to a height of 1·47 m. The entrance, which is in the NW sector, is spanned by two large lintels and is splayed externally. Immediately in front of the cell are the footings of a subcircular structure with a W-facing

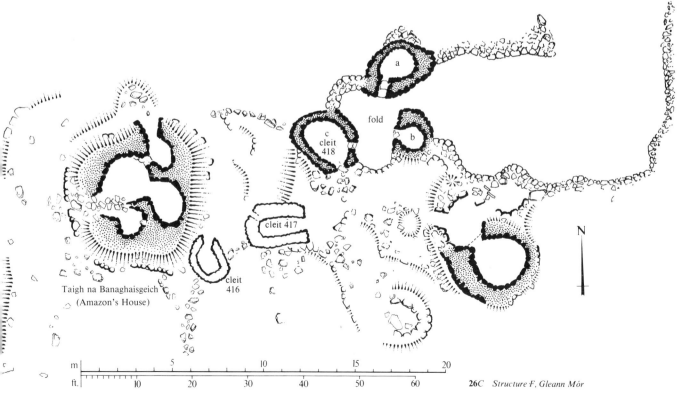

26C *Structure F, Gleann Mòr*

26D

26E

26F

26G

Structure F, Gleann Mór;
*   26D   cell c, entrance*
*   26E   SE cell from NW*
*   26F   'Amazon's House' from N*
*   26G   'Amazon's House', interior*

entrance. To the NE are traces of a smaller cell, and a short distance to the SW is a subcircular foundation with an internal diameter of about 1·37 m.

Further down the slope, to the W of the two cleitean (416–17), is a large mound containing a group of inter-communicating corbelled cells, of which one retains its roof. This structure has been known since at least 1697 as the House of the Female Warrior ('Taigh na Banaghaisgeich'), though by the 19th century it was referred to as the big sheiling ('Airigh Mhór').

On the N flank of the mound an outward-splayed entrance, 0·48 m wide, leads into a small ovoid cell which is 1·7 m in length and retains the remains of a corbelled roof rising to a height of 0·76 m above floor-level. In the W flank is a short passage, now blocked by fallen stones, which formerly gave access to a large oval cell 2·7 m in maximum length. A surviving 1·67 m stretch of wall-face in the N sector shows that the cell was probably corbelled, and stony debris on the S side conceals an entrance to a passage which intercommunicates with a third cell, a large lintel and parts of the jambs of the entrance still being visible. This cell is almost circular on plan, 1·22 m in diameter, and its corbelled walls rise to a height of 0·99 m. There is evidence of an entrance on the W side. In the E flank of the mound there is an entrance to a fourth cell, also of ovoid plan and measuring 1·93 m in length. The walls are corbelled and the crown of the roof is 1·58 m above floor-level. Above the door-lintel there is a 'window' or gap 0·46 m wide and 0·21 m high.

Around the base of the mound, especially on the S side, there are visible stretches of slightly battered wall-face. Of the two cleitean to the E of the 'Amazon's House', Cleit 416 is ovoid on plan, measuring internally 2·08 m by 1·17 m and 0·91 m in height. The doorway, which is at the N end, and the front of the cleit, have partly collapsed. Cleit 417 is rectangular on plan, its long axis aligned with the hill slope. Internally, it has a length of 2·54 m, a width of 0·81 m, and a height of 1·04 m. The entrance is at the E end, and there is a drain or vent in the rear wall.

— See Introduction nn. 61–2.

27   Structure G, Gleann Mór
NA 0876 0110   NA 00 SE 1
Occupying a sloping site below Structure F, this complex group comprises a 'gathering fold' and, to the W, a ruinous mounded structure of 'Amazon's House' type, which has been partly remodelled to form a cleit (414).

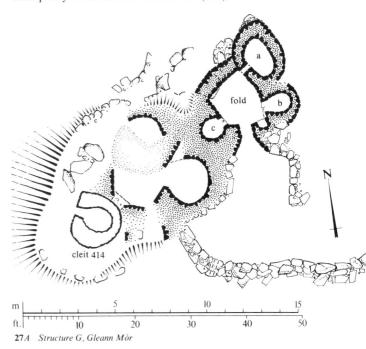

27A   Structure G, Gleann Mór

The fold consists of a roughly oblong open area, measuring 2·9 m by 2·54 m and enclosed by a vertical drystone wall up to 1·22 m high. It is fronted by a pair of stone dykes, and is associated with three corbelled cells (a–c). The entrance faces S and has an outward splay, measuring 0·66 m in width at the inner end. Immediately E of the entrance there is an aumbry 0·46 m wide and 0·76 m

27B *Structure G, Gleann Mór, from E*

above floor-level. A drain runs through the NW wall of the fold which abuts the outer wall of Cell *b*.

Cell *a* measures 1·22 m in length by 0·65 m transversely, and is entered by an aperture 0·56 m wide and 0·48 m high. The crown of the corbelled roof is about 0·86 m above floor-level. The corresponding internal dimensions of Cell *b* are 2·16 m by 1·07 m, its entrance-passage being 0·38 m wide and 0·33 m high. There is also a blocked external entrance at the N end. The corbelled roof rises to a height of 0·71 m above floor-level. Cell *c* measures 1·37 m in internal length by 0·91 m transversely. Its entrance is 0·38 m square and its corbelled roof rises to a height of 0·84 m above floor-level.

The area to the S of the fold is enclosed by low stone dykes, one running southwards from the E side of the entrance, the other extending eastwards from the outer wall of the 'Amazon's House'-type structure. Towards the W end there is what appears to be a drainage-channel beneath the wall.

The remains of the structure of 'Amazon's House' type consist of a stony mound up to 1·2 m high surrounding a central hollow area. Short stretches of inner and outer wall-faces are visible and contain what may be a blocked entrance on the S. A short arc of walling to the N is not obviously related to the main mound.

One roughly circular cell, over 2 m in diameter, was entered from the E side of this central hollow. It has a corbelled roof, which reaches a height of 0·94 m above the level of stony debris, and at the NW end there is a lintel spanning a cavity over 1·7 m deep. To the N, the remains of a second cell are represented by an arc of slightly corbelled walling 0·91 m high and 1·83 m long. On the SW side of the hollow there is a lintel surmounting a S jamb and wall-face. This has probably been an entrance to an original cell that has been otherwise remodelled to form Cleit 414.

Unusually, Cleit 414 faces W down the slope. It measures 1·88 m by 1·07 m within walls up to 0·94 m thick, its corbelled roof rising to a height of 0·86 m above floor-level. It was probably closed by the slab that is now in the entrance. At least two earthfast stones around this structure appear to have been reddened by exposure to heat, and a coarse potsherd was found inside.

28   Structure H, Gleann Mór
NA 0875 0110   NA 00 SE 1

This stony mound, which lies a few metres from Structure G, is the lowest of the linear group of structures running down the slope on the E side of the glen. Although very ruinous, enough survives to show that it has been a

structure of 'Amazon's House' type, subsequently dismantled to form two cleitean (412–13). Two re-used stones in Cleit 413 show traces of fire-reddening.

A subcircular area measuring 3·05 m by 2·9 m is surrounded on three sides by walls which stand to a height of 0·81 m and incorporate the E ingoing of an entrance to the S. The remains of at least two, and possibly four, cells can be discerned. To the N of the main area and at a slightly higher level, one cell has a wall-face 0·7 m high forming three sides of an area roughly 1·6 m square. To the NE of the main area and about 1·05 m above it, there is a subcircular cell with a diameter of 1·98 m. It is surrounded by a wall which survives up to 0·51 m in height and contains entrances in the NE and W sectors. An arc of stones probably represents the remains of a third cell to the N, and there are also vestiges of a small circular cell to the W of the main area.

Cleit 412 stands on the NW edge of the site and its doorway faces SE. It measures 2·87 m by 0·86 m wide within walls 0·76 m thick. The corbelled walls are spanned

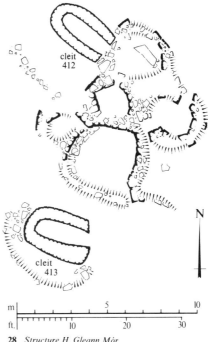

28   *Structure H, Gleann Mór*

53

by ceiling-slabs 0·86 m above floor-level. The cleit has evidently been used for storing cut turf, and was probably closed by the two large slabs that lie close to the doorway.

Cleit 413, which stands at the S end of the site, is 2·9 m long by 0·91 m wide within walls up to 0·84 m thick. The walls, which are corbelled, are ceiled by slabs 1·12 m above floor-level. Above the lintel of the doorway, which faces SE, there is a small window, and two of the three slabs in front of the entrance were probably used to close the doorway-opening. The cleit has been used for storing turf.

29 Structure J, Gleann Mór
NA 0872 0019   NA 00 SE 1

This well-defined 'gathering fold' overlying earlier remains stands on relatively level ground on the E side of the glen. It consists of a walled area, or fold, off which open three corbelled cells (a–c). On the NE side the fold is fronted by two curving stone dykes which vary from 0·6 m to 0·9 m in height and enclose an outer court.

The fold is of roughly ovoid plan, 3·6 m by 2·9 m, and the enclosing drystone wall, which has a vertical inner face, stands to a height of 1·22 m. The entrance, which faces NE,

is 0·61 m wide, and is flanked by walls up to 0·71 m thick. There is a channel or drain under the external face of the W wall.

To the W of the entrance, on the N angle, is Cell a, which measures internally 1·93 m by 1·22 m. It is entered through an aperture 0·48 m wide, about 0·58 m high, and 0·25 m above ground-level. Its corbelled roof rises to a height of 0·86 m above floor-level. Cell b, which is attached to the SW side of the fold, measures 1·65 m by 1·6 m internally, its entrance being 0·41 m wide, 0·48 m high, and 0·43 m above ground-level. Its corbelled roof rises to a height of 1·07 m above floor-level. Cell c, on the SE angle of the fold, was inaccessible for survey, the door-lintel and part of the N wall having collapsed. Its length appears to be between 2·1 m and 2·4 m, the entrance being about 0·43 m wide, 0·38 m high, and 0·43 m above ground-level. Its corbelled roof rises to an estimated height of about 1·1 m.

To the S and W of the fold there is an area of stony debris which, to the W of Cell b, incorporates an arc of low walling with an internal diameter of about 1·52 m. Between Cells b and c there is also a small subcircular area 1·02 m in diameter. Other sections of wall-face are visible but overall the surface remains do not form a comprehensible plan. It is reasonably clear, however, that they represent a structure which has been partly reconstructed to form a 'gathering fold'.

30 Structure Q and Well, Gleann Mór
NA 0879 0012   NA 00 SE 1

Lying below the steep slope of Mullach Mór, a little to the N of Structure F, this structure consists of a walled area flanked by two smaller 'cells', and has the appearance of a small and ruinous 'gathering fold'. None of the walls survives to a height of more than three courses (about 0·62 m).

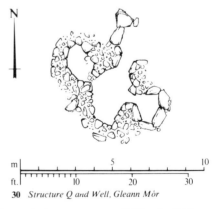

30 *Structure Q and Well, Gleann Mór*

The central area measures 2·59 m by 2·16 m and the entrance is at the NE end. The flanking SE 'cell', which is constructed of large boulders, measures approximately 1·52 m by 0·97 m with an intercommunicating passage 0·36 m wide. The surviving part of the outer wall-face of the NW 'cell' defines an area measuring 1·75 m by 1·3 m.

A little to the N and set in to the hill slope is a small well covering a spring. The well-cover consists of a lintelled drystone box 0·48 m wide, 0·48 m high, and 0·58 m deep. Although not so neatly or substantially built as Tobar nam Buaidh (NA 0865 0025), this well is more conveniently placed to serve the group of structures in this vicinity.

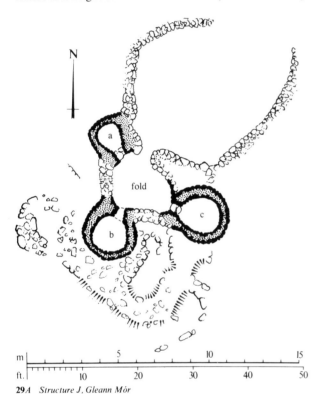

29A *Structure J, Gleann Mór*

29B *Structure J, Gleann Mór, from NE*

54

Boreray and Stac Lee

ST KILDA, THE NATIONAL TRUST FOR SCOTLAND AND THE WORLD HERITAGE CONVENTION

Trevor A Croft, The National Trust for Scotland

In 1972 the member states of UNESCO (United Nations Educational, Scientific and Cultural Organisation) unanimously adopted a Convention with the aim of ensuring the proper identification, protection, preservation and presentation of the world's most significant cultural and natural heritage. The Convention provided for the compilation of a World Heritage List of sites by the World Heritage Committee, which was set up to administer the Convention. It was always intended that this List should be relatively short – hundreds rather than thousands – and that it should contain only those properties, cultural or natural, or a combination of both, which are unquestionably 'of outstanding universal value'.

In December 1985 the United Kingdom Government submitted nominations to the World Heritage Committee, a list of seven sites which it considered fulfilled the criteria for inclusion in the list. The one Scottish property contained in this submission was the St Kilda archipelago, and its nomination was prepared on behalf of the Secretary of State for Scotland by the National Trust for Scotland, the Nature Conservancy Council, the Countryside Commission for Scotland and the Historic Buildings and Monuments Directorate of the Scottish Development Department. St Kilda was nominated because of the special significance of both its cultural and its natural heritage.

Following the visit of a UNESCO representative and a meeting of the World Heritage Committee in November 1986, St Kilda was placed on the World Heritage List, and in August 1987, at a special ceremony held in the island church, Mr Bernd von Droste, Director of the Ecological

Sciences Division of UNESCO, unveiled a plaque to commemorate the listing.

St Kilda is remarkable not only for its physical splendour and important seabird colonies, but also its history of human habitation, which is recorded so vividly in this volume. This history of St Kilda, which has a special place in the national consciousness, is itself of universal cultural significance. It is a story of the struggle of a small island community fighting for survival. The fact that it held out until 1930 is remarkable enough. But there is tragedy in the fact that a community which had survived the remoteness and physical hardships for so long should finally succumb to the influences of modern civilization.

The story is made all the more dramatic by its physical setting, for the St Kilda archipelago contains the most spectacular cliff scenery in Britain. The northern face of Conachair on Hirta falls away in a precipice almost 430 metres high, and the smaller islands of Boreray and Soay both have sheer cliffs over 360 metres in height. The two great sea Stacs, Stac an Armin (196 metres) and Stac Lee (165 metres), are the highest in the British Isles.

This awesome environment provides a haven for vast seabird colonies, one of the largest concentrations in the North Atlantic, and the seabird breeding population, which includes gannets, guillemots, razorbills, kittiwakes, fulmars and puffins, is undoubtedly the most outstanding wildlife feature. Less numerous, but no less significant, are the subspecies of wren and wood mouse found only on St Kilda, while the feral Soay sheep are descendants of the most primitive domestic form in Europe.

Village; St Kildans and Houses 3–6, 1886

The national importance of St Kilda in all these respects is recognised in its designation not only as a National Nature Reserve but also as a National Scenic Area and as a Site of Special Scientific Interest, while the main areas of the built heritage are protected under the Ancient Monuments Acts.

When the National Trust for Scotland accepted ownership of St Kilda in 1957, following a bequest from the 5th Marquis of Bute, there was an existing agreement to lease about three hectares of ground to the Royal Air Force as a base for tracking missiles fired from a newly developed rocket range on South Uist. The Trust decided that through ownership it could minimise the impact of this development, and further protection was given by leasing the islands to the then Nature Conservancy. The limits on military activity as set out by the lease have been assiduously observed by the Ministry of Defence, which also greatly assists the continuing programmes of conservation and research through the provision of logistical support.

The co-operation between the Trust, the Nature Conservancy Council and the Ministry of Defence has been a fine example of conservation in action, and the inclusion of St Kilda in the World Heritage List is fitting testimony to the success of this partnership.

GLOSSARY

Black house. A thick-walled, unmortared and thatched Hebridean house (Gaelic, *taigh dubh*, 'black house', or *taigh tugha*, 'thatched house').

Cleit (pl. *cleitean*). A small drystone building used for storage (Gaelic).

Consumption dyke. A thick wall built or enlarged to absorb ('consume') stones from the surrounding land.

Crùb. (1) Bed-recess in the thickness of the wall.
  (2) Wall-post of a jointed cruck (Gaelic).

Dyke. A drystone or turf wall (Scots).

Harr-hung. Of a door, hinged by pins fitting into sockets in the sill and lintel.

Ingo, ingoing. In architecture, the return face of a wall, usually where it forms the inner side of a doorway or window-opening.

Lazy-bed. A spade-built ridge used for cultivation, especially for potatoes.

Lot. A piece of ground allotted to a tenant.

Pintle. In joinery, a fixed pin or bolt associated with a turning member.

Planticrue. A small gateless enclosure for raising cabbages or kail.

Rubble. Masonry of rough unsquared stones.

Rybat. A side-piece of dressed stone in a window or door.

Sarking. Boarding laid on the rafters as a base for the roofing-material (Scots).

Stell. A walled enclosure for animals (Scots).

INDEX

Bold numerals in parentheses refer to article numbers in the Descriptive List.

Acland, Sir Thomas Dyke, traveller, pp. 2, 3, 4, 17; figs. pp. 2, 3.
Airigh Mhór, *see* 'Amazon's House'.
Altar, fig. p. 29.
'Amazon's House', pp. 2, 26, 27, 50–2 **(26)**, 53; figs. pp. 1, 26, 27, 50, 51, 52.
Ammunition-store, p. 17.
An Lag Bho 'n Tuath, pp. ix, 15, 23–5; figs. pp. 1, 23–5.
Arrowsmith, Aaron, cartographer, p. 33 (n. 9).
Atkinson, Robert, naturalist, p. 13.
Australia, p. 4.

Barn, pp. 19, 41–2 **(9)**; *see also* **Kiln-barn.**
Barra, p. 3.
Beinn a' Chaisteal, Islay, p. 33 (n. 65).
Bell, p. 36.
Benbecula, pp. vii, 49.
Black houses, pp. ix, 6, 7, 13, 21, 37–43 **(4–11)**; figs. pp. 4, 12, 13, 20, 38, 39, 40, 41, 42, 43.
'Boat-shaped settings', pp. 23, 25; fig. p. 25.
Boreray, pp. vii, x, 2, 29, 31; figs. pp. 1, 3, 29.
Bothies, pp. 2, 28, 29, 31; figs. pp. 29, 30.
Breakish, Skye, p. 37.
Brougham, Lord, traveller, p. 3.
'Buaile Crothaidh', *see* 'Gathering folds'.
Building construction: corbelling, pp. 23, 27, 28, 43, 44, 46, 47, 49, 52, 53, 54; floors, p. 19; masonry, drystone, pp. 28, 33 (n. 62), 38, 40, 41, 42, 44, 45, 46, 47, 48, 50, 52; roof structures, pp. 23, 42; figs. pp. 12, 20; *see also* **Building materials.**
Building materials: clay, p. 38; cobbles, pp. 35, 43; concrete, pp. 19, 37; felt, pp. 7, 13, 19; glass, p. 39; iron, pp. 21, 39; leather, p. 29; lime, pp. 19, 35, 37, 38, 42; mortar, pp. 19, 35, 37, 38, 42; plaster, p. 37; rope, pp. 3, 23; slate, pp. 35, 38; straw, p. 3; tar, pp. 7, 19, 39, 42; thatch, pp. 3, 6, 7, 13, 37, 42, 43, 44; timber, pp. 4, 35, 40, 42, 43, 46, 47; turf, pp. 23, 26, 27, 28, 29, 42, 45; wood, pp. 19, 23, 38, 40, 43, 46, 47; zinc, pp. 19, 37, 39.
'Bull's House', pp. 6, 37 **(3)**; figs. pp. 16, 37.
Burial-ground, pp. 6, 13, 15, 17, 19, 44, 45, 46, 48; figs. pp. 19, 22.
Bute, 5th Marquis of, landowner, pp. 13, 56.
Byres, pp. 21, 37 **(3)**; *see also* **Black houses.**

'Calum Mór's House', pp. 23, 44 **(13)**; figs. p. 44.
Campbell, Robert, surveyor, pp. 3, 33 (n. 9).
Cells, pp. 17, 21, 23, 27, 43, 44, 46, 47, 48, 49 **(24)**, 50, 51, 52, 53, 54; figs. pp. 49, 52; *see also* **Cleitean.**
Chapels, pp. 2, 17.
Chiesly, Rachel, *see* **Grange,** and **'Lady Grange's House'.**
Christ Church, p. 17.

Church, pp. 16, 17, 21, 33 (n. 33), 35–6 **(2)**; figs. 34, 35, 36, 37.
Cist-burial, p. 49.
Cleitean, pp. ix, 4, 6, 7, 13, 15, 17, 21, 28, 29, 31, 37, 42, 43–9 **(12–23)** 50, 51, 52, 53, 54; figs. pp. 19, 28, 29, 43, 44, 45, 46, 47, 48.
Cleitean McPhaidein, fig. p. 29.
Clettraval, North Uist, p. 49.
Consumption dykes, pp. 15, 42; *see also* **Dykes.**
Crosses, cross-marked stones, p. 17; fig. p. 19.
Cultivation remains, pp. 23, 25.

Doors, pp. 29, 40, 46, 48; figs. pp. 41, 48.
Drains, pp. 35, 38, 39, 40, 42, 43, 49, 52, 54.
Dykes, pp. 15, 23, 26, 27, 42, 49, 50, 53, 54; figs. pp. 1, 14; *see also* **Consumption dykes** *and* **Head dyke.**
Dumfries, Lord, *see* **Bute,** 5th Marquis of.
Dùn, pp. vii, 1, 2, 29; figs. pp. x, 1, 28.
Dunvegan, pp. 4, 33 (n. 32).

Earth-house, *see* **Souterrain.**
Enclosures, pp. 4, 6, 13, 15, 17, 23, 26, 37, 42, 47, 48; figs. pp. 1, 14, 25.
Excavations, archaeological, pp. 21, 23, 33 (n. 54), 37–8, 48–9.

Factor's House, pp. 4, 6, 7, 16, 17; fig. p. 17.
Ferguson family: pp. 13; Donald, 39; Neil, 39.

'Gathering folds', pp. 28, 50, 52, 54.
Gillies family: pp. 38, 40, 42; John, 42; Mrs John, senior, 13; Neil, 13.
Gleann Mór, pp. ix, 2, 15, 25–8, 29, 31, 50–4 **(25–30)**; figs. pp. 1, 26–7, 50–4.
Glebe, pp. 7, 16, 17.
'Gnocan sithean', p. 49.
Grange, Lady, pp. 23, 45; *see also* **'Lady Grange's House'.**
Grant, Captain Patrick, p. 1.
Greenock, p. 36.
Grenitote, North Uist, p. 37.
Gun, pp. 16, 17.

Harris, pp. 1, 2, 31, 33 (n. 32).
Head dyke, pp. 2, 4, 7, 15, 17, 23, 26, 42, 44, 46, 47, 48.
Hirta, pp. vii, 1, 2, 15, 25, 29, 31; figs. pp. x, 1, 28.
'Horned structures', p. 27.
Houses: pp. ix, 2, 3, 4, 6, 15, 19, 23, 32, 33 (n. 9), 37 **(4)**; figs. 11, 12, 18, 19, 20, 38; early houses, pp. 21–3; fig. p. 22.
'House of the Fairies', *see* **Souterrain.**
'House of the Female Warrior', *see* **'Amazon's House'.**
'House of the Staller', Boreray, p. 2, fig. p. 29.

Islay, p. 33 (n. 65).

Jetty, pp. 4, 16, 17; figs. pp. 1, 17.

Kearton, Cherry, naturalist, p. 49.
Kiln, kiln-barn, pp. 19, 42–3 (**11**).

'Lady Grange's House', pp. 23, 45–6 (**17**).
Landing-places, p. 17; figs. pp. 2, 3.
Lazy-beds, p. 25.
Lochinver, p. 41.
Locks, wooden, p. 21; figs. p. 21.
Loom, weaving, fig. p. 13.

Macaulay, Reverend Kenneth, missionary, pp. vii, 2, 3, 4, 15, 17, 25, 29, 31.
MacCrimmon family: pp. 21, 42; Effie, 42; Mary, 42; Rachel, 21.
MacDonald family: pp. 37, 41; Calum, 41; Lachlan, 37.
MacDonald, Reverend John ('Apostle of the North'), missionary, p. 33 (n. 33).
MacGregor, Alastair Alpin, journalist, p. 13.
Mackenzie, Reverend Neil, minister 1829–43, pp. vii, 2, 3, 4, 15, 17, 19, 23, 25, 29, 44, 49; infants, pp. 17–19.
MacLeod family: pp. 33 (n. 32); of Harris, 2; of MacLeod, 33 (n. 32); Captain Alexander, 33 (n. 32).
MacQueen, family: pp. 42; Donald, 42; Finlay, 13; figs., pp. 12, 32.
Manse, pp. 16, 17, 33 (n. 33), 35–6 (**2**); figs. pp. 34, 36.
Manure houses, manure pits, pp. 4, 29.
Martin, Martin, traveller, pp. vii, 2, 3, 17, 19, 27, 28, 29, 31.
Mathieson, John, antiquary, p. 49.
Mill, p. 19.
Monro, Donald, Dean of the Isles, p. 2.
Muir, T. S., ecclesiologist, p. 21.

Northern Isles, pp. 15, 23.
North Rona, p. 33 (n. 53).
North Uist, pp. vii, 23, 37, 49; *see also* **Uists**.

Orkney, p. 23.

Planticrues, p. 15.
Population, pp. 4, 13, 31, 32.
Post Office, fig. p. 11.
Pottery, p. 49.

Quern-stones, pp. 13, 19; figs. pp. 13, 39.

Rossinish, Benbecula, p. 49.

St Brendan's (Brianan's) **Chapel**, p. 17.
St Columba's Chapel, p. 17.
Sands, John, antiquary, pp. 2, 23, 48, 49.
Saw-pit, p. 4.
School, pp. 7, 16, 17, 35–6 (**2**); figs. pp. 35, 36, 37.
Scott, Betty ('Betty Scott's Cottage'), pp. 4, 21, 41 (**8**); figs. 20, 41.
Settlement-patterns, pp. vii, 2, 15–17, 25–6.
Sharbau, H, surveyor, pp. 4, 15, 19, 21, 33 (n. 21), 35, 39, 41, 42; figs. pp. 5, 6.
Shielings, p. 25.
Sibbald, Sir Robert, antiquary, p. 2.
Skye, pp. 3, 31, 37.
Slipway, p. 17; fig. p. 17.
Smallpox, pp. 31, 32.
Soay, p. vii; figs. pp. x, 2, 29.
Souterrain, earth-house, pp. 1, 2, 23, 48–9 (**23**); figs. pp. 22, 48, 49.
Stac an Armin, pp. x, 29, 31; figs. pp. x, 3, 29.
Stac Lee, pp. x, 29, 31; figs. pp. x, 3, 29, 30.
Stevenson, Robert, engineer, pp. 17, 33 (n. 33), 35.
Stone circle, p. 2.
Storehouse, pp. 4, 16, 17, 35 (**1**); figs. pp. 34, 35.
Stores, pp. 17, 21, 29; *see also* **Storehouse**.
'Streets', pp. 2, 17, 42, 45.
Structures, pp. ix, 21–3, 33, 50–4 (**25–30**); figs. pp. 27, 50, 51, 52, 53, 54.

'Taigh an t-Sithiche', *see* **Souterrain**.
'Taigh na Banaghaisgeich', *see* **'Amazon's House'**.
'Taigh Stallar', *see* **'House of the Staller'**.
Terrace-way, pp. 23, 43.
Thomas, Captain F W L, antiquary, pp. 4, 21, 28, 33 (n. 21), 41.
Tobar Childa, pp. 2, 15, 37, 47; fig. p. 22.
Tobar nam Buaidh, pp. 26, 54; fig. p. 26.
Travellers, pp. 1, 2, 3, 13, 17, 21, 23, 27, 28, 29, 31.

Uists, pp. vii, 1, 23, 31, 37, 49.

Valentines, Dundee, photographers, p. 7.
'Viking house', p. 19.
Village, pp. ix, 15, 17, 19, 21, 29, 31, 33 (n. 9), 34–49 (**1–24**); figs. pp. v, 1, 2, 5–20, 22, 30.

Wall-beds, pp. 3, 4, 21, 41, 48, 49; fig. p. 4.
Water-power, p. 19.
Wells, pp. 2, 54; *see also* **Tobar Childa**, **Tobar nam Buaidh**.
Windows, p. 39; figs. pp. 13, 39.

End-map: Village and An Lag Bho 'n Tuath; contoured plan.

Printed in Scotland for HMSO by (3093)
Dd 0 287061/HF 4694 C40 7/88